COMPUTER BASICS

CREATING A WEB SITE

How to build a web site in a weekend and keep it in good shape

Bruce Durie

GW00493706

LIGHTS CAMERA ACTION!

How To Books

BROMLEY PUBLIC LIBRARIES	
01942612	
H J	07/12/98
005.72	£8.99
	BH

Cartoons by Mike Flanagan

British Library Cataloguing in Publication Data
A catalogue record for this book is available from the British Library.

© Copyright 1998 by Bruce Durie.

Published by How To Books Ltd, 3 Newtec Place,
Magdalen Road, Oxford OX4 1RE, United Kingdom.
Tel: (01865) 793806. Fax: (01865) 248780.
email: info@howtobooks.co.uk
http://www.howtobooks.co.uk

All rights reserved. No part of this work may be reproduced or stored in an information retrieval system (other than for purposes of review) without the express permission of the Publisher in writing.

Note: The material contained in this book is set out in good faith for general guidance and no liability can be accepted for loss or expense incurred as a result of relying in particular circumstances on statements made in this book. The law and regulations are complex and liable to change, and readers should check the current position with the relevant authorities before making personal arrangements.

Produced for How To Books by Deer Park Productions.
Typeset by PDQ Typesetting, Stoke-on-Trent, Staffs.
Printed and bound by Cromwell Press, Trowbridge, Wiltshire.

Contents

List of Illustrations

Preface

Everyone is on the World Wide Web these days – or so it seems. Individuals, companies, schools, colleges, hobby groups, museums, local authorities, voluntary agencies and governments – everybody wants a presence on the Internet and more specifically that part of it called the World Wide Web.

Somewhere between 20 and 30 million people worldwide are using the Web and it is set to become the communications medium of the twenty-first century, overtaking print, radio and television. But who creates these Web pages and Web sites? And how?

The answers are – someone like you, and very easily.

No special knowledge or equipment is required – if you have a PC, access to the Internet and some free time, this book will show you how to turn an idea into a Web site.

You may want a personal home page, a site for your club or group or an Internet resource for your business. The step-by-step information in the following chapters will take you there. Only connect!

Bruce Durie

Web Facts

SETTLE ARGUMENTS! AMAZE YOUR FRIENDS!! BE A HIT AT PARTIES!!!

The Web seems to have become the single most contentious topic of conversation, supplanting football and 'Who won the Derby in 1953?' as subjects most likely to make people fall out. You're bound to be asked, so here are some Web Facts. They probably aren't correct, or have been superseded by other information, but at least you can point to them in the book and say 'It says so here'.

WEB FACTS

- There are 12 million subscribers to on-line services.
- There will be 100 million Internet hosts by 2000.
- There will be 150 million Internet subscribers by 2000.
- Electronic commerce will be worth £100 billion by 2000.
- There are 1,500 Internet service providers worldwide.
- There are 13,000 Internet mailing lists.
- By 2000 you won't need a PC to be on the Web. Internet hardware that plugs into your TV and cable will cost less than £60 and will be given away, like mobile phones.
- Over 37 million adults in the USA and Canada have Internet access.
- Over 55 per cent of Internet users are aged between 21 and 30.
- Over 93 per cent are male.
- Almost 70 per cent live in North America.
- Half describe themselves as professionals, and 22 per cent as graduate students (the two largest categories). The Net and the Web are growing at the astounding rate of 15 per cent per month.
- Monthly e-mail traffic went from 279 million in November 1992

to more than one billion at the end of 1993.

- The Web is also getting more international. Before CERN invented the Web, 95 per cent of sites were in America. Now Europe and Asia have 25 per cent of the sites. World Wide Web indeed.

- More than 4,000 new UK households subscribe to the Net each week.

- More than 3 million UK homes have a PC but no Internet access.

- Of those who use the Net, two-thirds use it primarily for e-mail, half for business information and only 6 per cent purchase goods and services.

- BT was losing 30,000 residential customers a quarter to the cable companies in 1995.

- Nearly a quarter of BT's business lines are ISDN, and it's growing at 5 per cent per year.

- AltaVista claims to cover 16 million Web pages and 13,000 Usenet groups.

- Lycos says it adds 700,000 new URLs per month.

- By the end of the century you're more likely to have a Web page than a car or a mortgage.

- The World Wide Web is primarily the creation of Tim Berners-Lee and Robert Cailleau, who, over a period from 1989 to the early 1990s, advanced the idea of a tool that would allow users to easily access Internet resources. This tool, called hypertext, provides a means for navigating.

- 25 per cent of Web users earn over £50,000 annually.

- 64 per cent of Web users have a university degree.

- Approximately 150 new businesses join the Internet every day ('Small Business Internet Usage to Double in 1996', *BIS Strategic Decision*, November 1995).

- 13 per cent of Internet users access the Internet on a daily basis (*Neilson Media Research*, 1995).

- Internet usage is expected to grow from 38 million users in 1994 to 200 million users by 1999 ('Making Mountains out of Molehills: Worldwide Internet User Market Forecast', *IDC*, April 1995).

- 2.5 million people have made purchases via the Web (*Neilsen Media Research*, 1995).

1
Getting Started

KNOWING WHERE TO START

Before you do anything else, read this chapter. Switch off your PC, get a pen and a notepad, put your feet up and read. This book will provide you with the tools you need to create a World Wide Web site over a few days. In this chapter you will learn:

- what software you will need
- how to set up your PC
- some of the technical jargon which is, unfortunately, necessary, since all jargon is a way of expressing a complex concept simply in a few words.

What this book does NOT assume
This book is not like those celebrity-chef cookbooks which start with a sentence like 'First, take your béchamel sauce...'. If you knew what a béchamel sauce was and how to make one, you wouldn't need that sort of cookbook.

What this book DOES assume
Rather this book assumes that you have:

- **Some experience** of 'surfing the Web', but it isn't essential.
- **No ability** in computer programming or desire to learn it.
- **Some knowledge** of the standard PC packages such as Windows and Word. (You may have other software – AmiPro for word processing, OS/2 as an operating system, Corel for graphics, Lotus Notes, etc., but this book makes no reference to these. However, it shouldn't be a problem.)
- **No ability** at graphic design (although if you do, your Web pages will probably look better).

- **No wish** to delve into the deeper recesses of communications hardware or software (yet!).

- **The need** to design, construct, test, implement and have up and running a decent, functional, good-looking Web site in a few days.

KNOWING WHAT YOU WILL NEED

In order to use this book you should already have these:

- a PC (*not* a Mac, Amiga or other non-PC type computer)

- Windows 3.1 (or 3. 11, also called Windows for Workgroups) or Windows 95 (also called Win95)

- a Web browser, ideally Netscape 3.01 or higher

- a graphics software package for handling images

- an Internet account with an Internet service provider (ISP).

Some information on all of these is given in the rest of this chapter. If you want to know more about computers, consult *How To Manage Computers at Work* or *Using the Internet*, both by Graham Jones, or *Buying a Personal Computer* by Allen Brown, both in this series. If you know all about this, apologies. If you are new to the whole field, here goes.

Choosing a PC

This book assumes you work on an IBM-compatible PC, not an Apple Macintosh (Mac), Amiga or other non-PC type computer. It is, of course, possible to design Web pages using these computers, but the software is different and this book does not deal with them. Most people use PCs at home and at work except professional designers, who prefer Macs. The latter became the *de facto* standard for graphic design and most designers are still joined to their Mac at the hip. But now PCs have caught up in terms of graphics handling and have remained cheaper. Macs will probably just go away, very soon.

Your existing PC
If you already have a PC it should be at least a 386 with at least 16MB of memory and 200MB free space on the C drive. A 486 or Pentium PC with 32MB of memory is better, since the faster the chip and the more the memory, the better and faster your Web pages will display.

Buying a new PC
If you are buying a new PC, make sure it is a Pentium 200 at least
and has 32MB of RAM, a hard disk of at least 1GB capacity, a CD-
ROM drive, a colour monitor and an internal or external 28,800 bps
modem (bps or bits per second is a measure of the speed at which a
modem can send information through the telephone system).

Free up some disk space
There are three reasons why you need lots of free space on the hard
drive:

- you will need space for some of the programs you will be loading

- you will need space for the files which make up your Web site

- Windows (see below) requires a fair amount of 'elbow room' for
  all the temporary files it creates.

If it isn't your own PC you are using, ask the owner or main user
before deleting any files to make free space!

Get a modem
If you haven't got a modem or a network connection you can't be
on the Internet. However, you could design a Web site on one non-
connected computer and import it into another one for uploading
to the server of your choice. If your boss catches you, it wasn't my
idea. The faster the modem the better – everything downloads
faster, cutting down your connection time and your phone bills. The
fastest modems available at present for normal purposes are 28,800
bps. This should cost less than £200.

Get a CD-ROM drive
At various times this book will tell you where to get free or cheap
software. If it comes off the front of a magazine, chances are it will
be on a CD-ROM. Most of the useful programs are, because as
programs, graphics, etc. get more and more complicated the amount
that can be shoe-horned onto a 1.44 MB floppy is getting severely
limited. Mind you, CD-ROMs have about another three years to go
before they are superseded by the next step in storage technology, so
buy a good one but not the most expensive thing on the market. Try
to get at least a quad-speed CD-ROM drive, although 16-speed is
obviously faster and if it can play audio CDs as well, you can have
entertainment while you work. This will cost £200 or less.

Choosing an operating system

Windows is the *de facto* standard operating system for PCs although if you have an IBM PC or certain others, your operating system may be called OS/2. This is similar enough to Windows for you to make sense of most of this book, but be aware that some of the software suggested for downloading may not work and a specialised OS/2 version should be sought out.

Which Windows version?

If you have an older PC, it is probably running under Windows 3.1 or 3.11 (also called Windows for Workgroups). Newer models will have Windows 95 (also called Win95). All of this book will assume you have one of these Windows versions, but you should know which. When programs are downloaded, the book will indicate whether to get the 16-bit (Windows 3.1/3.11) or 32-bit (Windows 95). The 16-bit/32-bit jargon refers to the speed with which the computer runs the programs and obviously Win95 is faster. Some software is written especially to take advantage of this, so there are often two versions of the same program. Make sure in each case you have the right one. Many 16-bit programs will work under Win95, but 32-bit versions will not work under previous Windows releases. If at all possible, operate in Windows 95. All the new software is being written with Win95 in mind so we must bow to the inevitable. Most of what is in this book applies to Windows 3.1 and 3.11 as well, and it will be made obvious if there are any differences.

Choosing a Web browser

The Web browser is the program which interprets Web pages and displays them and which also allows access to the Internet and the Web. If you do not have a browser, there is information in the next chapter on how to get one. The browser is capable of understanding and displaying HTML (hypertext markup language). HTML is not a programming language but a way of telling a computer what to display and how. Your Web pages will ultimately be written in HTML, but don't worry about that just yet.

Common Web browsers

The commonest browsers are Mosaic, Microsoft Internet Explorer and Netscape Navigator.

- **Mosaic**. Mosaic was developed by the NCSA (National Centre for Supercomputer Applications) in America as the first browser

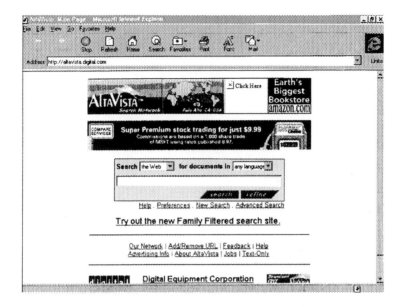

Fig. 1. Internet Explorer, Microsoft's Web browser, looks slightly different from Netscape Navigator (Figure 2). AltaVista is the searching tool shown here.

with a common interface for Windows, Macintosh and UNIX. There are various versions of Mosaic by companies who licensed the programming from NCSA – Spry Mosaic, Air Mosaic and others. It was the existence of Mosaic which made the Web popular and accessible. Netscape and Internet Explorer have taken Mosaic's principles further and largely supplanted it.

- **Internet Explorer**. Microsoft is as excited about the possibilities of the Web as everyone else and has produced its own Web browser, based on NCSA's Mosaic (above). Internet Explorer (see Figure 1) is readily available as it is given away free with magazines, pre-loaded on a lot of new PCs and generally made hard to avoid.

- **Netscape Navigator**. Netscape is the company which makes Netscape Navigator (usually just called Netscape) the most popular Web browser (see Figure 2). The first Netscape product was written by Mark Andreessen, the man responsible for Mosaic, after he was lured away from NCSA. There are various varieties of Netscape but get the latest one (currently Netscape

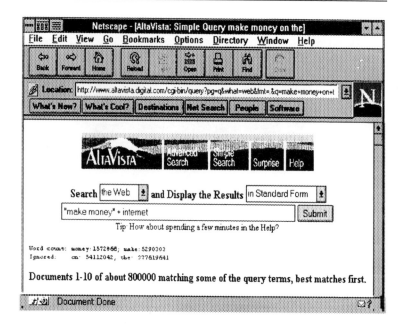

Fig. 2. This was a quick attempt at finding information on 'making money using the Internet' using Netscape as the Web browser and AltaVista as the searching tool. It found 800,000 items, which could have been cut down by refining the search terms. More of that later.

Navigator 3.04 but any version called 3.0x will do). This and other Netscape products can be downloaded with all the plug-ins as will be explained later. Avoid Netscape Communicator, a replacement but more complex product, for the time being. You can also get Netscape Navigator distributed on disk with computer magazines, although, like all shareware, you should have the decency to pay for it if you continue to use it after the evaluation period. Netscape has become the standard browser, despite Microsoft giving Internet Explorer away.

Which browser should you use?
That's up to you, but there are some things to bear in mind.

- They don't all do exactly the same thing – not all HTML commands work in all browsers since Netscape and Internet Explorer have created their own 'extensions' which can only be read by other people using the same browser. However, since Explorer is based on Mosaic and Netscape Navigator was written by someone who helped develop Mosaic, they're largely similar.

- You are likely to get one or other of these free – your Internet service provider (ISP – see below) may give you one of the browsers and encourage you to use it.

- Your Web page must be readable by others – the danger of only checking your work in one Web browser is that it just may not work in others. There is no reason why you cannot have different Web browsers on your PC and run them in turn to view your work.

- You are not stuck with one browser for ever – even if your service provider or PC vendor provided one of these free, you can change to another one if you wish or have more than one installed on your PC. This may require some fiddling.

- Java is on the way – Java is a new programming language which will revolutionise Web pages. It is not dealt with in this book. But others will put Java elements in their Web pages, so choose a browser that can read them.

- They will all be the same, eventually – possibly even by the time you read this, most browsers will support the same HTML extensions.

This book will concentrate mainly on the use of Netscape Navigator, so it would be advisable to have this browser. It has another great advantage – a built-in Web page editor, which this book will explain how to use to construct Web pages.

Choosing a graphics package

Graphics software will be required for handling images.

This book will suggest that you get **Paint Shop Pro** (PSP) which is an excellent graphics program that will do everything you want. It is also shareware (explained later). More complex tools exist (Photo Shop, Corel Draw, etc.) and when you have more experience, or if you are already using them, you may want to experiment. But whatever program you use, it *must* be able to create, import and export graphics files in a particular format known as GIF – files

which have names like myphoto.gif. Later in the book you will find
out how to acquire Paint Shop Pro.

Getting an Internet account

An account with an Internet service provider (ISP) allows you access
to the Internet and probably gives you an e-mail address. You may
already be registered with one of the large ISPs such as
CompuServe, America Online (AOL), Demon or Planet. Or your
workplace, school, college or local library may have a connection to
an ISP. If you don't have one, you can still create Web pages but you
will not be able to download software from the Web or upload your
pages to it. I once wrote an entire Web site on a fairly basic laptop
overnight in a hotel room with just Netscape and Paint Shop and no
Internet connection. It wasn't great, but it impressed the client that
it was possible. However, you may know someone with an Internet
connection who can get the required software for you and can
upload your pages later.

A service provider will give you a set of phone numbers you can
use to access their server, the software to do so and a bunch of other
goodies. Things to remember when making your choice are:

- **Monthly charge** – it typically costs £6–£15 per month for the basic
  service, which may come with five or ten hours free connect time.
  Watch out for ISPs who want the annual fee all at once – they
  may not be around long.

- **Connect time** – it will cost money (in most cases) to be on-line.
  Check the charges and how much connect time is free. A more
  expensive monthly charge may be cheaper if it comes with more
  free connect time. Remember that your phone bill will also go up.

- **Set-up charge** – some providers charge for their software.

- **Local numbers** – obviously dialling up your service provider costs
  phone time. Find out if the service provider has a POP (point of
  presence) in your local phone area or if there is a Freephone or
  Lo-call number. This will keep your costs down.

- **BT, Mercury, etc.** – If your phone line is not BT, can your service
  provider cope with this? It's best to check.

- **Free Web space** – there is little point in designing a Web page if
  there is nowhere to put it. Any number of people will offer you
  Web space but your service provider may allow you 1MB or more

free. Ask. Some magazines (like *.net*) offer free Web space if you subscribe.

- **Do you want Web access only** – larger service providers will have their own range of services in addition to Web access.

- **E-mail** – your service provider must offer e-mail services and, if possible, an e-mail auto-responder.

- **Support** – how good is their on-line and telephone support? You can waste a lot of time getting things wrong and not getting decent answers (or a busy phone line).

Knowing which service provider to use

Different people have different needs. If you are part of a local authority or group, or if you are working on a computer at a school, college or library, the decision may be made for you. Your company may have an account with a service provider. Individuals will have to subscribe to a service. However, a good strategy might be to sign up with almost anyone who offers a free trial, find out what's available, get as much information and download as much software as you can and then either stay with that provider or choose another one if you consider it better.

Places to start

The list is huge. Twelve of the most popular service providers are listed in Table 1, with their contact phone numbers (voice, not on-line) and costs at the time of writing, although the costs and benefits (such as free time) may change from time to time. This is not a recommendation for any of them, and others may be better for your purposes. A full list of UK service providers is available at *http:// www.limitless.co.uk/inetuk/table-provider.html*

Amongst the largest – and those most likely to provide free software and a trial period offer on a CD-ROM with a PC magazine – are:

- AOL – a European version of America On Line, the world's largest on-line services group with almost five million customers, but very US-focused. Access to the Internet is direct.

- CompuServe – second to AOL but with more non-US subscribers.

- MSN – the Microsoft Network, Microsoft's own, free software, which uses Internet Explorer as the standard browser (though this can be changed) and two sets of charges: hourly and unlimited.

Table 1. Service providers.

Service Provider	Phone number	Set-up charge	Monthly charge	Hourly connect charge	Free time (hours)
America On Line (AOL)	0800 279 1234	£0.00	£5.99	£1.85	5
Cityscape	01223 566950	£0.00	£7.99	£0.00	0
CompuServe	0800 454 260	£0.00	£6.70	£1.90	5
Demon Internet	0181 371 1234	£14.69	£11.75	£0.00	0
Direct Connection	0181 297 2200	£7.50	£17.63	£0.00	0
Easynet	0171 209 0990	£0.00	£6.70	£0.00	0
Internet Discovery	0181 6942240	£12.50	£15.00	£0.00	0
MSN (hourly)	0800 750 800	£0.00	£4.95	£1.95	3
MSN (unlimited)	0800 750 800	£0.00	£14.95	£0.00	0
Netcom	0800 973 001	£0.00	£15.22	£0.00	0
Nethead	0171 207 1100	£29.38	£9.39	£0.00	0
Pipex Dial	0500 474 739	£27.01	£17.63	£0.00	0
UK Online	0645 000011	£0.00	£9.99	£0.00	0

Be prepared to change
You can often try out a service provider for a month for free and change if you are not happy or find a better deal. However, if you have given out your e-mail number to all and sundry and you change service providers, you may have to let the world know your new address. Some providers will let you define an 'address for life' such as *mmouse@mmouse.co.uk*. Do ask.

UNDERSTANDING THE INTERNET AND THE WEB

It is worth taking time to understand some of the background to the Internet and the Web and equip yourself with some of the unavoidable jargon. You may be asked to explain it to friends and colleagues, or to justify your decision to have a Web site. A much fuller account is in *Using the Internet* by Graham Jones, in this series.

The Web isn't really there...Oh yes it is!

The Internet is nothing
The most amazing thing about the Internet is...it doesn't exist! It's

there, all right, and if you go by the incredible hype there has been recently for the Internet and the Web you could be forgiven for thinking it is some all-pervasive influence seeping into every corner of our everyday lives. Well, that's almost true as well. But the Internet does not exist as a single entity. There is no one place you can send a postcard to addressed 'The Internet', nor is there any front door you can go and knock on. The Internet is not a **thing** as such, more an **agreement** by a myriad of computers to talk together, share certain information and pass along almost any messages anyone puts into the system.

The Internet is everything
Asking 'What is the Internet?' is rather like asking 'What is the meaning of life?' – you will get as many different answers as people you ask, and no one answer is more correct or definitive than any other. It started as Arpanet, a method of routing communications via whatever computers were linked together in the event that a nuclear bomb or a terrorist attack took out some of the US defence computers and communications channels. However, it soon became the province of academics in universities who found it a convenient, fast and above all cheap electronic mailing mechanism.

Since then, a lot of other groups have come to use the Internet or at least hear about its potential. To academics and students, the Internet is a quick, easy and essentially free method of communicating with colleagues elsewhere (often in the office next door). To computer freaks, the Internet is an opportunity to 'surf' the 'information superhighway' (which doesn't exist either, by the way). To managers in businesses, the Internet is the biggest waste of employee time and phone bills since the speaking clock. To governments, the Internet represents the greatest threat ever to their control and power over information, even more so than free speech and cheap printing. To civil libertarians, the Internet is a great addition to personal freedom. To many parents, the Internet is an insidious, evil and above all **expensive** monstrosity, worse than arcade games. To many disabled people, the Internet is a lifeline and a window on the World.

Using the Internet as an opportunity
To you and me, however, the Internet is an unparalleled opportunity to find like-minded people, to share information, to promote and support our hobbies, to market our businesses and sell goods, services or information and to have a global letterbox – all

for very little cost and potentially huge returns. All you have to know is how to do it right.

Understanding the Web

The World Wide Web (the Web) is a graphical version of the Internet. It started life at CERN, the high-energy physics research establishment in Geneva, but is now available to everyone. It has the great advantage over other Internet mechanisms in being able to transfer more than just text. As a result, there is a need to design well for the Web since most people will view the output with a graphical browser (see below) and most likely in colour.

Making the Web work for you

The main steps to designing a basic Web page are these:

- Decide on the subject matter of your Web site – family, work, selling a product, information on a local group or activity, etc.

- Decide on the text, pictures and graphics you want in your Web page.

- Use a text editor to write the text and the commands that will make it work as a Web page.

- Edit and format any graphics you want to incorporate.

- View your Web pages on your PC with a graphical browser.

- Upload your Web site to a server via an account you have with an Internet service provider.

2
Getting the Software You Need

FINDING THE RIGHT SOFTWARE

To design your Web pages as described in this book you will need these programs:

- WinZip 6.2
- Netscape Navigator 3.01
- Paint Shop Pro
- Notepad.

In the case of the first three programs, they are the latest version at time of writing, but please resist the temptation to download later versions at the moment – programs can change their look, feel and even basic operations between release versions – since it will make following this book much harder. Once you know how to use them, feel free to get the very latest bells-and-whistles upgrades. If you have Windows, you should have Notepad (in your Windows directory), a simple text editor. Check whether your PC has the other programs listed above. If not, you should acquire them, initially as freeware or shareware.

UNDERSTANDING FREEWARE AND SHAREWARE

You will come across programs listed as freeware or shareware. It is important to understand what these terms mean and the difference between them.

Freeware
It's free. It's as simple as that. You can use it as much and for as long as you like and even, in many cases, pass it on to others in an unmodified form. Often, it has been written by an enthusiast with a

kind heart who believes that it will make life easier for the rest of the world. Sometimes the author asks for a donation towards the costs and it's up to you how you feel about that. Sometimes you can buy a more professional, upgraded or later version. But do read any disclaimers and legal notices that come with the software.

Shareware

This is a 'try before you buy' idea based on the concept that no one in their right mind will spend hard-earned money on a program that they don't like, doesn't work, isn't suitable or will never be used again. Shareware allows you to use the program and to pay for it later. Usually, it comes time-limited (30 days, say, or a certain number of times you can use it). Sometimes it automatically stops working after a period, sometimes it flashes up annoying 'remember to pay' messages after the expiry time and sometimes it just sits there and keeps working happily. However, when you first load it there will be some sort of agreement you will have to make that binds you to paying for it if you keep using it or intend to do so. Every time you use the program after a stated period you are breaking this agreement. Play fair, and pay up. The ultimate penalty is jail.

There are advantages to paying for it as well – you will probably get a manual, some enhanced functions, an update and a codeword, registration password or serial number that allows you to remove all the annoying reminder messages.

Evaluation and demo software

Often, the programs that come 'free' with a PC magazine are evaluation or demo versions. They may be effectively shareware, in that they are time-limited but if you decide to use them you can pay and get the real version. In some cases they are disabled in some way – you can't save or print, for instance, or only so many files can be created, or it will stop working after ten times. Again, paying brings advantages and the full version.

KNOWING WHERE TO FIND THE PROGRAMS

There are three main ways to get this software.

Getting a CD-ROM with a PC magazine

Programs distributed on computer magazine covers are widely available and often the easiest way to try out new software. But they are not always the best idea – they may be disabled in some way (see Evaluation and demo software, above), not unpack onto your computer properly or conflict with existing programs. However, the more reputable magazines take care to ensure that the software on their cover CDs is both workable and useful. Check back issues of magazines like *PC Direct*, *Computer Shopper* or any one of a dozen others to find the software you need. Often they have listed inside a back-issues telephone number or, in the more sophisticated ones, a Web address from which you can download some of the software.

Buying it from a supplier
A local computer store will be able to source almost any software for you and can often get it as freeware or shareware.

Downloading it from the Web
One of the nicely recursive things about the Web is that everything you need to make the best use of it is available from it. However, you can spend your life searching around only to find clogged-up download sites. Below are listed reliable sites (at the time of writing) where the required software can be accessed. But to make it easy for you, all the programs have been assembled for you at http://www.fifeweb.net – click on 'Downlands'. If a friend downloads software for you onto another computer, it may not be possible to transfer it easily onto yours, since most of these programs, even in compressed form, are bigger than the 1.44MB that will fit onto a floppy disc. (The answer is to use the Windows Backup program to get the files onto multiple floppies then use Restore to load them onto your PC. But even a compressed back up of 40MB of files may take 20 or more disks.)

Web addresses
If you would like to explore some download sites, here are the URLs and some instructions. The Web pages may have changed by the time you read this book, but these addresses should be a start at least. You can type the addresses directly into the Location box of your browser, as in Figure 3.

Fig. 3. The Location box of Netscape.

WinZip 6.2

WinZip is an 'unzipping' program. Many of the files you download will come with the extension .zip, which means they have been compressed to make them smaller and, often, to pack several files together into one compressed 'archive'. WinZip expands them, a process rather like pulling the rip cord on a parachute – the whole thing unpacks, becomes a lot bigger and starts to do its job. The URL is *http://www.winzip.de/com* Download WinZip 6.2 for Windows 95 as winzip95.exe or WinZip 6.2 for Windows 3.1 as winzip31.exe. Note that there may be alternate download sites available which are faster because they are closer to you, or less heavily used.

Netscape Navigator 3.01

Use this as your Web browser and as a Web page editor to create your pages. Even if you routinely use Microsoft Internet Explorer, please get Netscape Navigator as well since this book makes a great deal of reference to it. This is not the same as Netscape Communicator, a more complex combination of Navigator and other Internet software, which is best avoided for the moment. The latest version at the time of writing is 3.01. It can be downloaded from *http://live.netscape.com/comprod/mirror/client_download.html* using a form which asks for certain information and looks like Figure 4.

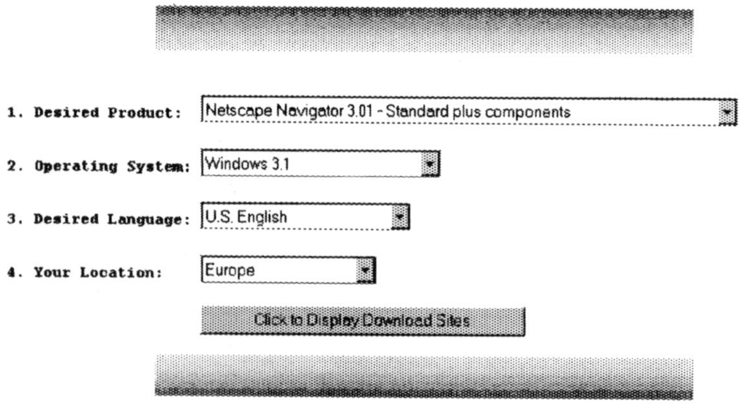

1. **Desired Product:** Netscape Navigator 3.01 - Standard plus components

2. **Operating System:** Windows 3.1

3. **Desired Language:** U.S. English

4. **Your Location:** Europe

Click to Display Download Sites

Fig. 4. Downloading Netscape.

Keep all the options as above, with the exception of Operating System, which will either be Windows 3.1, as here, or Windows 95. The file you download will be called something like g16e301p.exe (16-bit for Windows 3.1) or g32e301p.exe (32-bit for Win95). Once on your computer, double-click on the file name in File Manager or Windows Explorer to unpack and install it (see Installing the software, below).

Paint Shop Pro 3.11 or 4.14
This wonderful image manipulator is just the thing for handling all the gif files you will use in your Web pages. It may be all you ever need. You can get PSP directly from the authors, JASC, at *http://www.jasc.com/pspdl.html* or from the addresses below. As ever, make sure you choose the right version for your PC.

GifCon
Later, you may want to get this wonderful piece of software which lets you turn a series of gradually different images into an animation, exactly like sticking photographs together to make a movie. GIF Construction Set for Windows 95 is GIFCON32.EXE. and for Windows 3.1 and 3.11 is GIFCON.EXE. The URL is *http://www.mindworkshop.com/alchemy/gifcon.html*

Microsoft Internet Explorer
Should you wish to investigate Microsoft's Web browser, it can be obtained as Windows 95 and Windows 3.1 versions from *http://www.microsoft.com/ie/download/*

Other software
The only other program you need is Notepad.exe, which should be in the Windows directory or folder of your PC. However, you should make sure that your browser knows that this is your default editor. In Netscape, this (and your default graphics package) can be listed by clicking on Options Editor Preferences General, which brings up a dialog box as shown in Figure 5. (Your directories may not be the same as those shown.)

INSTALLING THE SOFTWARE

When you download the various software, it will usually come with installation instructions. These should be followed **to the letter** otherwise the program may not work. Individual installation

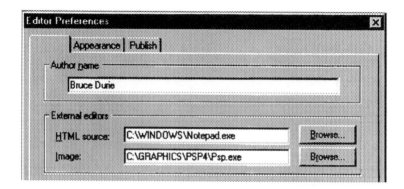

Fig. 5. Setting Editor Preferences in Netscape.

instructions are outside the scope of this book, but these programs have been chosen partly for their ease of installation and the quality of the instructions. In most cases downloading will deliver a single file which you should store in your c:\windows\temp directory – if you don't have such a directory, create one. Usually, the file will either have the file extension **.exe** or **.zip**. If it's an **.exe** file, it is self-extracting – just double-click on it and it will unfold for you if you follow the instructions. If it is a **.zip** file, open WinZip (which you downloaded first, remember?) and extract the file into a directory of your choice. Sometimes this produces a set of setup files and you must click on setup.exe or install.exe to get the actual programme. Read all installation notes carefully.

Checking for bargains

Every so often during your Web browsing you will come across a bargain – a free download of some new software to try out, for instance. Equally, the various computer magazines have CD-ROMs on the cover with demo or fully-working versions of authoring and other software. Do try any and all of these. It's only by experimenting that you will find what's best for you.

BEING CAREFUL

Some words of caution, however – if you are downloading and/or installing software, always do these three things:

• Back up important information regularly.

- Have a virus checker running in the background on your PC and in addition to that, check all CDs, floppies, etc. for viruses before doing anything else. Viruses are not as all-present as the newspapers would have us believe, but they do exist and one good virus can ruin your life for quite a while.

- Before installing any software whatsoever, close down every other application with the exception of the Windows 95 program itself (the Program Manager in Windows 3.1 and 3.11).

What next?
Now that you have all the software on your PC, unpacked and installed according to the instructions, you are set up and ready to go.

3
Writing Your First Web Page

TAKING YOUR FIRST STEPS

This chapter assumes that you have Netscape Navigator installed on your PC and a word processing program, preferably Word, plus Notepad.

In this chapter you will take your first steps towards writing and designing a Web page. But first you will have to decide whether you want to use a Web authoring tool, or to get into the wonderful world of HyperText Markup Language (HTML) directly.

There are three basic ways to construct a Web page:

- use a Web authoring tool (see below)
- write it from scratch using a text editor such as Notepad
- copy someone else's Web page and amend it.

Each of these has its advantages and drawbacks. This chapter will deal with Web authoring tools first, mostly in order to dismiss them.

Don't let anyone put you off

Everybody knows somebody who knows better. It's usually a brother-in-law, workmate or the man who props up the end of the bar, but they just know everything, don't they? And a surprising proportion of them are computer nerds. They know all about the Internet, were the first people on the planet to download the Pam Anderson pictures and have an opinion on every aspect of everything you do.

And you've probably said to them, or in their radar-like hearing, 'I fancy doing my own Web page'. This is usually met with one of those teeth-sucking, breath-indrawing, head-shaking routines typical of builders asked for a quote. And it was probably followed by 'Well, you'll have to learn HTML and it's damned tricky'. Well, you won't if you don't want to. And even if you did, it isn't.

UNDERSTANDING HTML

HTML is HyperText Markup Language. It is actually very accessible – almost intuitive – and, best of all, it isn't a programming language, more a set of styles and formats which the Web reads to display its information. Using HTML you tell the Web browser what text, fonts, colours, backgrounds, graphics, links, tables, forms and other features are in your Web page. It is really a form of desktop publishing. It has a small number of commands and instructions called 'tags' associated with it. These tags surround or precede particular aspects of your document and tell the browser they are to be handled in a particular way. Think of it as a document file with knobs on.

- HTML is constantly changing and improving with new tags being added all the time The latest standard at the time of writing is HTML 3.0, although Netscape, Mosaic and Internet Explorer all have non-standard 'extensions' to HTML which other browsers may or may not recognise.

- There is a lot of interest in HTML with the growth of the Web and a lot of support available on-line. A good place to start is The HTML Writers Guild with free membership, 6,000 members in 45 countries and a great deal of free help, advice and software. Contact the Guild on *http://www.hwg.org*

Web pages are easy
This book contains most of the standard HTML you will ever need and tries to get you to do things by HTML as much as possible. But it is very straightforward. There is no need to go learning new tricks especially when there are clever people out there making better and better software that save you the bother.

We have the technology
There was a time when you needed a degree in rocket science to perform simple arithmetic calculations on a computer. Now there's probably a spreadsheet on your computer more sophisticated and powerful than the program that controlled the first space mission. Likewise, there are powerful tools that can help make Web page construction easier.

WEB AUTHORING TOOLS

If you really don't want to get into HTML there are authoring tools which can do it all for you, if you can use a word processor. You can turn your Word for Windows (and some other word processing software) into an HTML package by bolting on an authoring tool such as Microsoft Internet Assistant. Others are mentioned below.

What to do if you're not using Word

Most decent word processing packages allow you to save a file as HTML. If not, save it as a text file and open it using Netscape Editor, as described below.

Realising that you don't need authoring tools

HTML editors and authoring tools are fine and every one has its advantages and drawbacks. The choice is a very personal one, like the car you drive or the newspaper you read. But the real truth is, you don't need any of them at all. If all you wanted out of your Web page was to reproduce some document in a Web-friendly format (and that's what a lot of Web pages are) you could just import it into Word with Internet Assistant loaded, mark it up and save it as an HTML file. This process will compose an HTML header and do other Web-friendly things for you.

But nobody really wants to read words alone from a computer screen. It is very boring. HTML can add navigation links within the document, hyperlinks to other HTML documents and Web sites, graphic images and various types of multimedia including audio, video and 3-D. If you really want control over your Web page construction, all you need is Notepad, a decent graphics package and some add-ons freely available on the Web. Most of this book assumes exactly that. HTML documents are basically text files and can be created, edited and saved by using Notepad, the simple text editor that comes with Windows. Notepad is not a clever program, but it is fine for writing HTML.

USING INTERNET ASSISTANT

Internet Assistant is essentially a set of templates for Word (see Figure 6). It uses styles, macros, macrobuttons and hidden text to do what it does. You 'mark up' the text by selecting it and using a toolbar icon or drop-down menu to change plain text to markup tags. You can even include in-line GIF images (a particular type of

Fig. 6a. This is how Word 3.11 looks in normal Word mode.

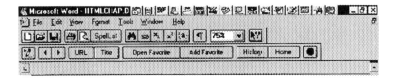

Fig. 6b. And this is how Word 3.11 look in Web browser mode (click on View web Browse).

graphic file developed for CompuServe for just this purpose, but we will deal with that later). All the time you are working in the Word format you know and love. You then save the file as an HTML document with the file extension .htm. However, it is a text file which can be edited with Word or Notepad. That means if you know how to use Word, you are nine-tenths there with your Web page authoring. Other authoring tools can be templates for word processors or stand-alone HTML editors.

Starting with a Word document

Your Web page is bound to have text in it, probably quite a lot. Now you're ready to create your first HTML document. You will do so by starting with a normal Word document, since that's what you're used to, and converting it to HTML.

Open a new file using the normal.dot template and type in this text exactly as it is here. Notice that it refers to pictures you will add later.

THIS IS MY WEB PAGE

My name is (*put your name in here*) and I live at (*your address*).

Here is a picture of me.

I hope you like my Web page. If so, e-mail me at the number below:
j.smith@email.com (*put your own e-mail address here if you have one;
if not type it as here*)

If you want to know more about me, click on this *link*.

Here's where to get software

Thank you for paying attention.

Sickening, isn't it? But it's a start. Make sure the title line is bold and a larger type size and that the word *link* is in italics. Save it as myfile1.doc. Make sure you save it as a Word document (with a .doc extension).

Now save that document again as an HTML file using $\underline{S}$ave $\underline{A}$s. You will notice that Word calls it myfile.htm. The appearance will change to something like this:

THIS IS MY WEB PAGE
My name is (*name*) and I live at (*address*).
Here is a picture of me.
I hope you like my Web page. If so, e-mail me at the number below:
j.smith@email.com
If you want to know more about me, click on this *link*.
Here's where to get software
Thank you for paying attention.

Some of the formattings don't translate across. Don't imagine your lovingly crafted Word document looking the same on a Web page. Sometimes you will convert a Word document, happily save it as HTML and when you reopen it, the look has changed. The HTML save did not retain some of the Word formats. So it is worthwhile closing and reopening documents regularly to check they look like you imagine they should.

WORKING WITHOUT INTERNET ASSISTANT

All the above could have been achieved by just using Netscape Navigator's Editor function and Notepad. Try this:

- Make sure you have a directory or folder called c:\myweb – create it with Windows Explorer or File Manager.

• Start Netscape (off-line – without accessing your phone line via the modem, and you may need to click the red STOP button).

• Click on File New Document Blank – this opens the Editor.

• Type in the THIS IS MY WEB PAGE text given earlier.

• Save it as myfile1.htm in your c:\myweb directory.

• Click on File Browse Document – this shows you what it will look like as a Web page.

• Go back to the Editor with File Edit Document.

• Click on View Edit Document source – this will open Notepad, but your browser may ask you to specify this.

• It will look something like this:

```
<!DOCTYPE HTML PUBLIC "-///W3C//DTD HTML 3.2//
EN">
<HTML>
<HEAD>
<TITLE> THIS IS MY WEB PAGE</TITLE>
<META HTTP-EQUIV="Content-Type" CONTENT="text/
html; charset=windows-1252">
<META NAME="Generator" CONTENT="Microsoft Word
97">
<META  NAME="GENERATOR"  CONTENT="Mozilla/
3.04Gold (Win95; I) [Netscape]">
</HEAD>
<BODY>
<DIR>
<P><FONT SIZE=-1>THIS IS MY WEB PAGE </FONT></P>
<P><FONT SIZE=-1>My name is (put your name in
here) and I live at (your address). </FONT></P>
<P><FONT SIZE=-1>Here is a picture of me.
</FONT></P>
<P><FONT SIZE=-1>I hope you like my Web page.
</FONT></P>
```

```
<P><FONT SIZE=-1>If so, e-mail me at the number
below: j.smith@email.com
</FONT></P>
<FONT SIZE=-1>If you want to know more about me,
click on this link.
</FONT></P>
<P><FONT SIZE=-1>Here's where to get software
</FONT></P>
<P><FONT SIZE=-1>Thank you for paying attention.
</FONT></P>
</DIR>
</BODY>
</HTML>
```

- Exit from Notepad *without* saving. You were only looking.

That was a great deal easier than using Internet Assistant. Where Internet Assistant is really useful is in converting an existing Word document into HTML format. However, Word itself can save a file as .htm with a lot of the formatting intact.

ORGANISING HEADS AND BODIES

What the example above shows is the basic structure of any HTML document. At the very least it *must* have the following:

```
<!doctype html public "-//W3C//DTD HTML3.2//
EN">
<HTML>
  <HEAD>
    </TITLE>. . .</TITLE>
  </HEAD>
<BODY>
</BODY>
</HTML>
```

Notice that:

- Some of these tags are paired, the second one (with a "/") being a closing tag.

- `</HTML>. . .</HTML>` surrounds the entire document.

- Tags containing a "!" at the front are not displayed – they are comments. The tag `<!doctype html public "-//IETF// DTD HTML//EN">` tells the browser that it is an HTML document and conforms to a certain Document Type Definition that you needn't worry about.

- The `</HEAD>. . .</HEAD >` tags surround all the header information and *must* contain a title surrounded by `</TITLE>. . .</TITLE>` Everything else is contained within `<BODY>. . .</BODY>`

CREATING HYPERLINKS IN WORD DOCUMENTS

Hyperlinks are clickable signposts to hypertext references (HREFs) which are other documents or places within a document. Clicking on the hyperlink will take you to where the hyperlink points. There are three type of links you can put into your document using the Insert HyperLink command. We will make hyperlinks to a local document, a URL, and a graphic.

Linking to a local document
The local document must be on the same (local) hard drive as your myfile.htm document.

1. Save your myfile.doc document as myfile.htm

2. Open a new file using the HTML template.

3. Type 'Hello World' into the new file.

4. Save As Hellow1.htm into your C:\myweb directory and close the file.

5. Back in myfile.htm, select the word 'link' in the line 'If you want to know more about me, click on this link'.

6. Insert Hyperlink and make sure it is to Local Document called Hellow1.htm. The word link is now blue and underlined, indicating a link.

7. Save the file.

8. Change to Web Browse view.

9. Click on the word link and watch Hellow1.htm open.

10. When you've finished admiring it, close Hellow1.htm. You have just created your first hyperlink.

Linking to a URL

URL stands for Uniform Resource Locator and is the path name of a file, document or graphic, which fully describes its position on the Internet. Examples might be:

http://www.netscape.com,/index.html
ftp://ftp.newserver/ftp.file

The part of the URL before the colon and double forward slashes identifies the server type or transfer protocol. The rest is the location name. URLs are case-sensitive, so be careful with upper and lower case. To keep it simple always use lower case throughout URLs.

1. Save your myfile.doc document as HTML.

2. Make sure you are in Web Edit view.

3. Select the word 'software' (in the line 'Here's where to get software').

4. Insert Hyperlink to URL. When it asks for a file to link to, type (or select) http://www.microsoft.com. (This is just a convenient URL. In reality you would choose one you actually wanted to go to.)

5. The word 'software' is now blue and underlined, indicating a link.

6. Save the file.

7. Change to web Browse view.

8. Click on the word software. You will get a message saying the file can't be found, but that's just because you're not on-line.

Linking to a graphic

You can both link to a graphic and use a graphic as a hyperlink.

1. Find a graphic that is in GIF or JPEG format. There must be one somewhere on your hard disk or on a CD or floppy you got with a magazine. An easy way to find out is in Windows Explorer or File Manager and search for *.gif or *.jpg. Find a relatively small one and copy it to your C:\myweb directory.

2. Place your cursor at the bottom of the document, before 'Thank you for paying attention' and Edit Bookmark. Give the Bookmark Name as PIC and click Add.

3. Insert Picture your GIF or JPEG file into the document at the same point as the bookmark. Click Advanced Sensitive Map. In the Alternative text box type No Image.

4. Select the word 'picture' in the second line.

5. Insert Hyperlink to Bookmark and select the PIC bookmark and OK. The word 'picture' is now blue and underlined, indicating a link.

6. Save the file and change to web Browse view.

7. Click on the word picture. Your file will jump to that picture (in fact, to the bookmark which is the anchor for the picture link). It could have been several pages away.

8. In Web Edit view, select the picture by clicking on it. Insert Hyperlink to Local Document and select Hellow1.htm. Click OK.

9. Make myfile.htm web Browse view and click on the picture. This will open Hellow1.htm. You have now linked a word to a graphic and a graphic to a local document.

10. Finally, in Web Edit view click on View Field codes and see what's actually going on. It may not make much sense, but at least it's all there.

Saving and browsing it

So that's your first Web page. Keep it on your hard disk for reference. You should now open your browser and load this file into it to see how it looks for real. In Netscape the command is File Open File. The links should be active and your chosen picture visible. Later you will see how to activate an e-mail link.

INVESTIGATING OTHER HTML EDITORS

Other programs you may want to investigate are HotMetaL, HotDog, HTML Assistant, webAuthor and Microsoft FrontPage, all of which are available as shareware or freeware, so you can try them before buying.

HotMetaL

SoftSquad at *http://www.sq.com* can provide you with a slightly disabled version of their HotMetaL which can be upgraded to HoTMetaL PRO 3.0 for a fee.

HotDog

Sausage Software provide HotDog free for a thirty-day evaluation from their Web site *http://www.sausage.com* If you like it, pay a registration fee. They can also be contacted at sales@sausage.com.

HTML Assistant Pro

This is a freeware, fully-functional HTML editor which can be used without registration for an unlimited period. More features are available in the commercial version which is available by sending your credit card details by e-mail to sales@brooknorth.com or via the Web at *http://fox.nstn.ns.ca/~harawitz/index.html*

webAuthor

webAuthor from Quarterdeck is among the more expensive editors, but the payment gets you a manual, Help file tutorial and three months technical support by phone. It spots syntax errors, supports Netscape extensions and has a custom dictionary of HTML, Net and Web terms. It doesn't understand Word document formatting, however.

FrontPage

This is Microsoft's companion Editor to Internet Explorer and is widely available.

FINDING OUT MORE

If you want to get into this further, consult webMaster which is a massive collection of tips, programs, information and resources about Web sites and HTML. The URL is: *http://gagme.wwa.com/~boba/masters1.html*

4
Making More of Text

HTML FORMATTING TAGS

The text in the last example was somewhat boring and you will be wondering how all those wonderful, colourful text effects you have seen in Web pages come about. The answer is in special text formatting tags you can use in your own Web pages. But first, a recap.

USING HEAD AND BODY TAGS

Three tags, <HTML>, <HEAD> and <BODY> will appear in every Web page HTML document.

```
<HTML>. . .</HTML>
```
The <HTML> tag tells the Web browser that the document is an HTML page. Put <HTML> at the top of every HTML document you write and </HTML> tag at the bottom of every document. Everything else happens between these tags.

```
<HEAD>. . .</HEAD>
```
The <HEAD> tag tells the browser what the document is called and that this part of the document is at the top. It should contain a title between <TITLE>. . .</TITLE> tags.

```
<BODY>. . .</BODY>
```
Everything else is the body, and goes between <BODY> tags. So a basic document might look like:

```
<!DOCTYPE HTML PUBLIC "-//W3C//DTD HTML 3.2//
EN">
<HTML>
<HEAD >
```

```
<TITLE>Terry's Home Page</TITLE>
  <META NAME="Author" CONTENT="Bruce Durie">
  <META NAME="GENERATOR" CONTENT="Mozilla/
  3.03Gold (Win95; I) [Netscape]">
</HEAD>
<BODY>
<P><B><FONT SIZE=+1>Terry's Very Own, Very
Special Web Site</FONT></B></P>
<P><B>This site is under construction</I></B>
</P>
<P>It will have information on </P>
<UL>
<LI><A HREF="bmx.htm">BMX bikes</A></LI>
<LI><A HREF="girls.htm">Rotten, yukky girls
</A></LI>
<LI><A HREF="raithrov.htm">Raith Rovers</A>,
the greatest football team ever</LI>
<LI>and what I had for my <A HREF="mytea.htm">
Tea</A></LI>
</UL>
</BODY>
</HTML>
```

The </HEAD> and </BODY> tags are used at the end of their sections to explain to the Web browser when that section is finished. Why bother? Because some browsers can't make sense of the HTML code without them.

This Web page, when viewed with a browser, will look like this:

Terry's Very Own, Very Special Web Site

This site is under construction.
It will have information on
BMX bikes
Rotten, yukky girls
Raith Rovers, the greatest football team ever
and what I had for my Tea

Don't laugh – a lot of Web pages out there are little more than this.

The underlining you see indicates hyperlinks – navigation aids to other Web pages or to other places in this Web page – and will be described later.

There is no need to insert all these tags manually, as Netscape Editor will do it for you. First you will recreate this document and then the HTML tags themselves will be explained.

1.   Open Netscape and click on File New Document Blank – this opens the Editor.

2.   Type in the text above, without worrying about formatting or tags.

3.   Save the file as C:\myweb\terry1.htm

4.   Make sure you have the three toolbars showing (see Figure 7).

5.   Use the Netscape Editor buttons to mark up the text (see Figure 8). Do this by marking a line of text – put the cursor at the beginning of the line, hold down the left mouse button and drag the cursor along. For instance:
     • make the first line bold and a larger font
     • make *This site is under construction* bold and italic
     • make the four content lines bulleted and indented
     • mark the words underlined in the example above and click on the Hyperlink button – when it asks for a Link, type in bmx.htm or girls.htm or raithrov.htm or mytea.htm – all lower case, notice. (These are all documents which don't exist yet.)

6.   Save the document and click on the Browser button. This shows the effect of your changes, which you don't see in the Editor.

7.   Go back to the Editor and View Edit Document Source – this will look like the HTML two pages back so compare this with the Editor buttons you used and see what Netscape did to provide the HTML tags. They are explained, with others, in the next section.

ADDING TITLE, HEADING AND PARAGRAPH TAGS

Title tags <TITLE>...</TITLE>

The title of your document is important because the title determines

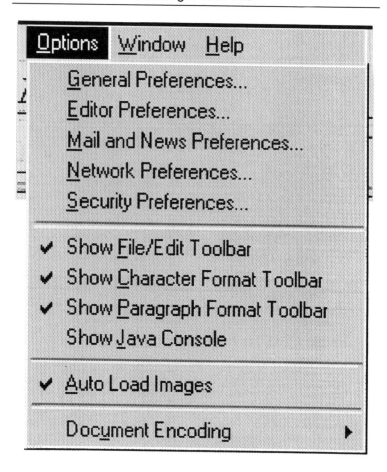

Fig. 7. Enabling the toolbar options.

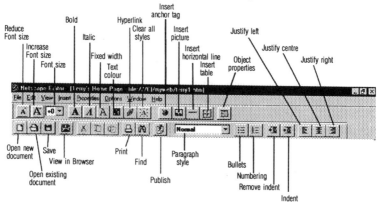

Fig. 8. The Netscape Editor toolbars.

the bookmark of a Web page when saved and is useful for search engines. It is not displayed when the Web page is browsed.

Terry's Very Own, Very Special Web Site

is not a *title*, but a piece of body text.

Heading tags (<H1> and </H1> to <H6> and </H6>)
Heading tags are font styles, and look something like this:

Heading1
Heading2

Heading3
Heading4
Heading5

Heading6

They are abbreviated, when used as tags, as <H1>Text</HI> and so on. Most people never use more than H1, H2 and H3.

You can achieve the same effect with < FONT SIZE=+1>. . .</FONT> which increases the size from the default (roughly equivalent to 12 point). Try changing the numeral (to +2 or -1) in Notepad, saving the document and browsing it to see the changes.

Line break tags <BR> and paragraph tags <P>
HTML files do not understand hard or soft line returns. Hard returns are what happens when you press Enter and soft returns (also called carriage returns as a hang-over from typewriter days) when you press the Shift and Enter keys together. However, any line breaks you enter into your Notepad document will not format like that in HTML. You must tell HTML when you want a line break and a paragraph space.

The line break tag, <BR> is the HTML equivalent of the soft carriage return. The paragraph tag <P> is like a hard return and inserts more space. To start a new line or paragraph, use <BR> or <P>, at the end of a line or paragraph or at the start of the next. Notice that <BR> does not have to be 'closed' like <TITLE> or <H2> – there is no </BR>.

<NOBR>Text</NOBR>

This means **NO BR**eak and all the text between the <NOBR> tags will not have line breaks in it. This is useful if you want a line (an equation or an address, perhaps) not to be broken up.

<WBR>

The **W**ord **BR**eak tag is useful in a NOBR section if you know exactly where you want it to break. Lines of poetry would be a good example. The <WBR> tag does not make a line break like <BR> but tells the browser where a line break can be allowed.

Text formatting tags

In HTML, text format tags can be physical (sometimes called visual) or logical.

Physical or visual markup tags are attributes you can easily see the effects of like *italic* (<I>Text</I>), underline (<U>Text</U>), **bold** (<B>Text</B>) or Typewriter fixed width font (<TT>Text</TT>).

Logical tags are styles used to emphasise a point or cite a source document and will, one day, do more than this. Some of these are:

- <ADDRESS>Text</ADDRESS> This is the style format for putting your address (jsmith(@server.org,uk) in a document. It's basically bold italic.

- <CITE>Text</CITE> For citing sources, references and so on as in *The Importance of Being Earnest*. Looks just like *italic*, doesn't it?

- <CODE>Text</CODE> Used to indicate programming code or equations, for example: 10 IF x=y+count then go to end. This is like the <TT> fixed-width font.

- <EM>Text</EM> Emphasis. *Go away!* Looks like *italic*, again. See STRONG, below.

- <KBD>Text</KBD> This is supposed to tell the user to make a keyboard entry: to register, type in **xx0012345-D**. This usually appears as bold fixed width.

- <MENU>Text</MENU> A small typeface, as in toolbar menu commands.

- <PRE> and <PRE WIDE> These styles put text into a fixed width font of various sizes and within a frame of a pre-defined size.

- <STRONG>Text</STRONG> Strong emphasis: Shut down your computer now! would be an example. It normally appears as bold.

- <VAR>Text</VAR> This represents a variable the users are supposed to replace with their own word. Example: OPEN *DATABASE* asks you to type in the name of the relevant database. Again, it tends to appear as italic.

Why so many text tags?

The question is: if they're all just variations of bold, italic and fixed-width, why bother? The answer is that as Web browser software gets cleverer, there will be new and better functions for these and other logical tags. When virtual reality gets going, <STRONG> will probably make a boxing glove come out of the screen and punch you. When logical tags actually do something they will be worth using. At the moment, they are a solution waiting for a problem. Notice that all these style tags have to be closed (<I>Text</I>).

Centring text

Don't ask me why, but whoever dreamed up HTML didn't think to include a way to centre text. Netscape, however, has provided an 'extension' (unofficial) <CENTER>Text</CENTER> tag as used in an example above. Remember the American spelling.

Adding a banner <BANNER>. . .</BANNER>

This is a very useful item which is used to enclose static text information to remain on display at all times. It is HTML 3.0, however, and may not be understood (yet) by your browser.

MAKING MORE OF FONTS

New extensions to Netscape can be used to modify font sizes.

<BASEFONT SIZE=value>

This defines the overall font in the document and all FONT changes (below) are relative to this. It defaults to 3, and has a range of -7 to +7.

<FONT SIZE=value>

Again, the default FONT size is 3 and the range is -7 to +7. This means a document could have a line like:

```
B<FONT  SIZE=+1>I<FONT  SIZE=+2>G<FONT
SIZE=+3>G<FONT SIZE=+4>E<FONT SIZE=+5>R
```

This would display as BIGGER

```
<FONT COLOR="value">
```

FONT can also be used to change the colour of text. This will be dealt with in more detail in the chapter on images and backgrounds.

```
<FONT FACE="face">
```

The actual typeface can be specified, for example: <FONT FACE= "Arial">

Be wary of specifying strange fonts this way – they need to exist on the computer of whoever is viewing your page and if they don't, the browser will choose the 'next best' font, which may throw out your carefully-conceived design. Stick to common fonts like Times and Arial wherever possible.

All <FONT...> tags can (and must!) be closed with </FONT>

You can use COLOR= and FACE= in <BASEFONT> too.

```
<BLINK>Text</BLINK>
```

This will make the enclosed text blink on and off.

CREATING LISTS

Don't use a line break tag <BR> or a paragraph tag <P> to create a list. Use the two list styles <UL> and <OL>.

Unnumbered Lists <UL> and List Items <LI>
If you typed in:

```
<UL>
<LI> Tea
<LI> Sugar
<LI> Milk
<LI> Biscuits
</UL>
```

you would have a very useful shopping list, with bullets:

• Tea

• Sugar

- Milk

- Biscuits

Note the Unordered or Unnumbered List tag, <UL>Text </UL> at the start and end of the list and the fact that each line starts with List Item tag <LI>.

Ordered Lists <OL>
For a numbered list, use the Ordered List tag <OL>Text</OL> again with <LI> at the start of each line. This would produce:

1. Tea
2. Milk
3. Sugar
4. Biscuits

Definition Lists <DL>Text</DL><DT> And <DD>
Later in this chapter (Anchors and Bookmarks) there is an exercise in which the sentence:

If I had a hammer, I'd hammer in the morning

takes the viewer to definitions of 'hammer' and 'morning'. If, for instance, you wanted to include a glossary or dictionary somewhere in your Web site you would enter the definitions of 'hammer' and 'morning' using a definition list <DL>, definition term <DT> and definition <DD>

```
<DL>
<DT> hammer
<DD> An instrument used for getting people out of
bed in the morning
<DT> morning
<DD> The bit of the day between falling asleep
and having your first coffee and aspirin, often
associated with hammer.
</DL>
```

Each definition term starts with a <DT> and each definition with a <DD>. There's now a <DL> at the start and a </DL> at the end. The <DT> and <DD> entries can have paragraphs (separated by <P>) tags).
  Definition Compact <DL COMPACT> has the same effect but in a

slightly smaller typeface, just as a book index or contents page is often in a smaller type than the body text of the book.

Directory Lists `<DIR>Text</DIR>`
This puts a directory-style list in your HTML document and is a useful way of creating information columns. Type your list, such as:

J Smith	01444 222333	Chum
R Brown	01555 111000	Boss
G George	01666 444999	Father

Each entry can be in a separate paragraph. Use a tab between items in a line. Sometimes Internet Assistant has trouble with this and puts them all on separate lines each starting with a `<LI>` when you view the list in Netscape. Edit your code manually to stop this nonsense.

The `<BLOCKQUOTE>` tag
Say you wanted to quote something that runs over a few lines, like a poem.
    `<blockquote >` If I should die, think only this of me
    There is some corner of a foreign field
    That is forever England... `</blockquote>`
    `<P>` (What a load of old Tosh).`<P>`

This would display as:

```
If I should die, think only this of me,
There is some corner of a foreign field
That is forever England...
```
(What a load, of old Tosh).

Use line break tags, `<BR>` to separate the lines.
    There are other formatting styles like PRE (preformatted) and MENU.

DRAWING HORIZONTAL LINES `<HR>`

It's called `<HR>` not `<HL>` because it refers to Horizontal Rule, a typesetter's term. The `<HR>` tag draws a line as wide as the browser window and the width can be controlled with

    `<HR WIDTH=X%>`

where X is the percentage of the screen width the rule should occupy. <HR WIDTH=100%> takes up the whole screen, <HR WIDTH= 50%> half of it, centred. To make the rule thicker, include SIZE=Y, where Y is the number of pixels. Try viewing the document source and adding <HR WIDTH-100%> and <HR WIDTH= 20% SIZE-20> as the last two commands in an HTML document. Notice there is no closing tag for <HR>.

ADDING SPECIAL CHARACTERS

The following signs are reserved for special functions. HTML uses these characters for certain aspects of markup tags. You know about < and > already, as the tag brackets.

< (called left angle bracket or 'less than' sign)
> (right angle bracket or 'greater than')
& (the magnificent ampersand)
" (double quote)

There will be some awkward individuals out there – myself amongst them – whose lives won't be complete unless they can use these characters for some normal, textual purpose. You might want to include a line of an equation that looks like this:

IF x < 2 > y & proc1 = "OFF" then "blah!"

But HTML wants these characters, so you can't have them, at least, not without some special trickery in the shape of escape characters. This also goes for accent marks. You may be familiar with the use of codes called escape sequences to get special characters into Word or DOS documents. If you ever wanted to put the following characters into the text of an HTML document, here's how:

for <	type < &lt >
for >	type < &gt >
for &	type < &amp >
for "	type < &quot > (or forget " and use a single quote instead)
for ^{TM} (Registered Trademark)	type < &reg >
for © (Copyright)	type < &copy >

In fact, you can type them directly into Netscape Editor, but if using Notepad, you must use the special character method. There are others, which can be found at *http://www.w3.org*

CREATING HYPERLINKS IN DOCUMENTS

Hyperlinks are clickable signposts to hypertext references (HREFs) which are other documents or places within a document. They look like this in HTML: <A HREF=. . . . .>Text</A> and appear in Web browser like this: **Text**.

Clicking on the hyperlink will take you to where the hyperlink points. There are three type of links you can put into your document using the Insert Link command or the Hyperlink button. We will make hyperlinks to a relative link (a local document), a remote URL and a bookmark anchor.

Linking to a local document
The local document must be on the same (local) hard drive as your terry1.htm document.

1. In Editor, open a new blank file.

2. Type 'I like BMX bikes' into the new file.

3. Save As bmx.htm into your C:\myweb directory and close the file.

4. Browse terry1.htm, click the Reload button (to let the browser know the file has changed) and click on the BMX link – this takes you to the linked document and you can return to terry1.htm by using the browser's Back button (top left).

5. Notice that the words BMX bikes are now a different colour and underlined, indicating a link that has been followed. You can change the look of these by clicking on Properties Document.

6. You have just created your first hyperlink. When you've finished admiring it, try creating girls.htm, adding some text of your own, and seeing if it works.

Linking to a URL
URL stands for Uniform Resource Locator and is the path name of a file, document or graphic, which fully describes its position on the internet. Examples might be:

http://www.netscape.com/index.html

ftp://ftp.newserver/ftp.file
or, the one you'll be using here, *http://www.raithrovers.com/*

The part of the URL before the colon and double forward slashes identifies the server type or transfer protocol. The rest is the location name. URLs are case-sensitive, so be careful with upper and lower case. To keep it simple, always use lower case throughout URLs.

1. Open terry1.htm in Netscape Editor.

2. Put your cursor somewhere in the words Raith Rovers.

3. Click on Properties Link (or click on the Hyperlink button) – when it asks for a file to link to, type *http://www.raithrovers.com/*

4. Save the file, change to the Browse view and click on Reload.

5. Next time you are on-line (your modem switched on and connected to a phone line) clicking on the Raith Rovers will take you to that URL. If you are not on-line, you will get a message saying the file can't be found.

Linking to a graphic
You can both link to a graphic and use a graphic as a hyperlink. Find a graphic that is in GIF or JPEG format. There must be one somewhere on your hard disk or on a CD or floppy you got with a magazine. An easy way to find out is to use Windows Explorer or File Manager and search for *.gif or *.jpg.

1. Find a relatively small one and copy it to your C:\myweb directory.

2. Place your cursor at the bottom of the terry1.htm page in Editor after 'Tea'.

3. Use Insert Image to place your GIF or JPEG file into the document at the same point as the cursor. Click on the Link tab to check that it is still linked to mytea.htm – if not, type this in.

4. Save the terry1.htm file.

5. Open a new blank document and use Insert Image to put your picture into a new file – save this as mytea.htm and close it.

6. Back in terry1.htm change to Web Browse view and Reload.

7. Click on the image – your browser will jump to mytea.htm, which

contains the picture. Of course, it could have been another picture – this is often used to place a thumbnail (small version of the picture) in one Web page and link it to a larger picture that takes up a page on its own – and we can do this, too.

8. With terry1.htm in Editor view, click on the picture to mark it, then click Properties Image – you can now play around with the size, whether or not it has space round it and so on. Save whatever you decide.

9. Open mytea.htm in Editor and click on the picture – make it bigger by altering the Height and Width.

10. You have now linked a graphic to a local document which itself contains a graphic.

11. Finally, with terry1.htm in Editor click on View Edit Document Source to see what's actually going on (you may have to save it first). It may not make much sense, but at least it's all there.

Linking to an anchor

You can use a hyperlink to help you move around a page.

1. Place your cursor at the very start of the terry1.htm page in Editor, before 'Terry'.

2. Use the Insert Target button to bring up the Target properties box and type in top (lower case) – notice the target symbol which appears.

3. Place your cursor at the bottom of the terry1.htm page in Editor after 'Tea' and your image.

4. Press the enter key to make a new line and type the word 'Top'.

5. Mark the word 'Top' and click on the Hyperlink button – it may still be linked to mytea.htm so type this in or select the target top from the Current document. Notice that it appears as #top, which is how you know it is an anchor.

6. Save terry1.htm, change to Web Browse view and Reload.

7. Click on the word Top – didn't do anything, right? That's because the browser is taking you back to the top of the page, which you can already see.

8. With terry1.htm in Editor view, add some extra lines of text – it doesn't matter what – before 'This site is under construction'

until the word Top disappears below the foot of the page, and Save.

9. Browse the document and Reload – now when you click on Top the browser will jump back to the top of the page.

10. Finally, with terry1.htm in Editor click on View Edit Document Source to see the HTML.

11. Experiment with other anchors – 'bottom' is an obvious one, but you may call them almost anything you like and put them anywhere. You could, for instance, insert an anchor called Raith before Raith Rovers and put a link to it elsewhere on that page.

You could also put an anchor in another document – mytea.htm, for instance – and make your hyperlink from Tea point to a specific place in the mytea.htm file. In this case you would place an anchor in the mytea.htm file and edit the Link associated with Tea in terry1.htm to link to a target in a Selected file (in this case mytea.htm).

Using links to send information

Later in this book you will see how to activate an e-mail link and use it to send a message or other information to a remote site.

FINDING OUT MORE ABOUT HYPERLINKS

You will have used these already in examples earlier in this book to link a Web page to a point in itself, another Web page or a completely separate URL elsewhere. Hypertext is far and away the strongest feature of HTML. It does this by use of an anchor tag and hypertext reference, hence the syntax < A HREF > . Every anchor tag must have:

*   the anchor code < A HREF = ... >

*   the linked file or URL name

*   the link text

*   the closing tag < /A > .

An example would be <A HREF="http://www.microsoft. com">/Microsoft Support Team </A>

The <A HREF=. . . . . .> element takes the link to the URL of the Microsoft home page. The phrase **Microsoft Support Team** will appear in the HTML document as underlined text in a different colour, indicating a link. </A> closes the tag. The linked URL could be almost anything on the Internet – a Web site, an FTP server, an e-mail address or another HTML document. The characters before the colon and double slash (://) tell the browser what kind of entity the linked site is.

Linking to other URLs
The common ones you will come across are:

```
<A HREF="http://. . . . . .">link</A>
```
a Web site

```
<A HREF= "mailto:. . . . .">link</A>
```
sends an e-mail (note no //)

```
<A HREF= "ftp://. . . . . .">link</A>
```
an FTP site, usually for downloading software

```
<A HREF= "news:. . . . .">link</A>
```
a newsgroup, for downloading articles

```
<A HREF="telnet://. . . . .>link</A>
```
an outside (non-Internet) network

```
<A HREF="gopher://. . . . .">link</A>
```
a gopher site

The text before </A> is whatever word, phrase or image is highlighted and which activates the link when clicked. For the record, ftp stands for File Transfer Protocol and http for stands for HyperText Transfer Protocol, which are instructions to your browser on how to connect.

Linking to specific bookmark
If there is no identifier, as in <A HREF="homepage.html"> link</A>, this indicates an HTML document in the same folder or directory.

The presence of a hash (#) sign indicates a bookmark somewhere in the same or another Web page:

```
<A HREF="#PIC">link</A>
```

```
<A HREF="nextpage.html#PIC2">link</A>
<A HREF="www.kingston.ac.uk/index.html#help">
link</A>
```

UNDERSTANDING MORE ABOUT ANCHORS AND BOOK-MARKS

This section is for those who wish to delve deeper into hyperlinks, anchors and bookmarks.

Since a link can be another piece of text elsewhere in the same HTML document, it can be used to construct a list of definitions at the end of your Web page. You could include at the start of the document:

If I had a hammer, I'd hammer in the morning

Each of the instances of hammer would be a hyperlink inserted as:

< A NAME = "#hammer definition" > hammer < /A >

and morning might be:

< A NAME = "#morning definition" > morning < /A >

At the end of your document you would have:

< A NAME = "hammer definition" > < /A > An instrument used for getting people out of bed in the morning.

and morning might be:

< A NAME = "morning definition" > morning < /A > The bit of the day between falling asleep and having your first coffee and aspirin, often associated with hammer.

The # means a link within the same document (see above).

If your definitions were in a separate document, you would use the same tag but with the file name (defdoc.htm, say) added:

```
<<A HREF="defdoc.html#hammerdefinition"> ham-
mer</A>.
```

The browser will now go to defdoc.htm first before looking in there for the appropriate # anchor.

SUMMARY

That's your first Web page. Keep it on your hard disk for reference and remember the following:

- Use Netscape Editor to construct your pages.

- Continually save and Browse the file to see how it really looks – you may have to click the Reload button.

- Do as much markup as you can using the Netscape Toolbars, but check the Document Source in Notepad to see what the HTML codes are – if you alter these manually, save the file, close Notepad and save the document again in Netscape Editor.

- Make certain alterations (such as changing the font face from Times Roman to Arial directly in the Document Source HTML

FINDING OUT MORE ABOUT HTML

A very good source of lots of useful information including guides to HTML can be found at: *http://www.bev.net/computer/htmlhelp/*

5
Brightening Up Your Pages with Backgrounds and Colour

ADDING COLOUR

Many Web pages are colourful and contain coloured text. You have come across one example of coloured text using the <FONT COLOR=. . . > tag, but there are other ways too, by using specific 'attributes' within the <BODY. . . > tag which have 'parameters' or 'values'.

Using Netscape Editor
The easy way to add colour in Netscape Editor is to use Properties Document Appearance. This will allow you to change text and background colours. Appearance Background gives you a palette of at least 48 colours to play with. Try some of these on one of your existing Web pages, but watch these points:

- Make sure that the background colour does not obscure the text colour. For instance, your hyperlink text colour may stand out but your Active link colour may not.

- White text on a black background looks very striking, but until the background loads, you'll have white text on white. If the background never loads, for some reason (such as someone's unusual browser doesn't support backgrounds), it will seem that your web page is empty.

- If you have images on your page, check that they work against the chosen background colour and that if the image is transparent (see Chapter 6), the background doesn't obscure any detail.

- Some colours harmonise and others clash. More detail on this plus some basic rules for choosing colours are given in Chapter 10.

Using HTML code directly
Background can be added one of two ways:

61

1. using the background colour

2. using a specific image file of a certain colour – this gives more flexibility and control over colour effects.

Background colour
The following attributes can be added to <BODY. . .>. Notice that the American spelling (COLOR) is used throughout.

•   BGCOLOR – the background colour (HTML 3.0 and above):

```
<BODY BGCOLOR="#RRGGBB">............</BODY>
```

The colour definitions (like #RRGGBB or #C0C0C0) are explained below in Specifying Colours.

•   BACKGROUND – this defines an image to be used as background of the current document:

```
<BODY BACKGROUND="slate-grey.gif">......</BODY>
```

Normally, you would have the required GIF file in the same directory as your web document. But you needn't, provided you address it properly. The BACKGROUND attribute must have the URL or filename of the background image:

```
<BODY BACKGROUND="/images/this_image.gif"> or
```

```
<BODYBACKGROUND="http://www.colour.com/
images/that_image.gif">.
```

See below for specifying backgrounds not in your own c:/myweb directory.

Text colour
TEXT=   the colour of all the normal (body) text <BODY
         TEXT="#RRGGBB">............</BODY>
LINK=   the colour of links not visited yet
VLINK=   the colour of visited links – those the viewer has already
         clicked on
ALINK=   the colour of active links activated by clicking on them:

The colours for the three links can be combined as:

```
<BODY  LINK="#RRGGBB"  VLINK="#RRGGBB"
ALINK="#RRGGBB">.........</BODY>
```

An example would be:

```
<HTML>
<HEAD>
  <TITLE>Colour Example</TITLE>
</HEAD>
<BODY TEXT="#C0C0C0" BGCOLOR="#000055" LINK=
"#FF8000" VLINK="#3377FF" ALINK="#22AA00">
<CENTER><P>CHANGING BODY, LINK AND FONT COLOUR
</P></CENTER>
<P>This is an example of changing body link
colour and text colour within the body. </P>
<P>Text is light-grey on blue, and <A
HREF="terry1.htm">hypertext </A>is <FONT COL-
OR="#FF8000">yellow-orange</FONT> (FF8000),
<FONT COLOR=11#22AA00">green</FONT>(22AA00)
when activated, and <FONT COLOR="#3377FF">light
blue </FONT> (3377FF)if already visited. </P>
</BODY>
</HTML>
```

- Make sure whatever document you hyperlink to (terry1.htm, which you created in the last chapter) is in the same subdirectory (C:/myweb) as this document.

- Note that <BODY....> will only work once. If you have two <BODY....> statements in your HTML document, only the first will be acted upon.

- See below for FONT colours.

SPECIFYING COLOURS

The other attributes (BGCOLOR, TEXT, LINK, VLINK and ALINK) need to be told which colour value or parameter to use. This is either:

- a six-character hexadecimal (HEX) colour value (< BGCOLOR = "#RRGGBB" >) where RR is the Red value of the colour, GG the Green value and BB the Blue value. Each number can be from

0 to F (15 in Hex format). HEX value F4 is 15 x 16 + 4 = 244 in the decimal system. The possible values for each colour are 00 to FF, which is 255, making 256 specifications for each colour component and thus 256^3 (16,777,216) possible colours. How can you work out the HEX values? See Colour and HEX below.

or

• a colour description, which Netscape will allow (e.g. < BGCOLOR = "Red" >). It is not easy to find out exactly which colour descriptions are permitted. Try some and see what happens.

Colour and HEX
To find out what the values for a colour should be, use this cheat:

1. Open MS Paint or a similar painting package.

2. Double-click on any colour shown in the bottom tool bar and click Define Custom Colours or a similar command.

3. Clicking on any colours shown will give you the colour values for that colour. Orange, for instance, is Red 255, Green 128, Blue 64. These are in decimal, of course, not HEX. (In Paint Shop Pro just place the cursor over any colour you see and the RGB values will be shown, but in decimal.)

Converting decimal to HEX
To convert to HEX, open your Windows Calculator. Click on View Scientific. Type in any number (169, say) and check the HEX circle. It will change 169 to A9 (HEX for 10 is A and 10 x 16 + 9 = 169). This is the value you want.

MAKING BACKGROUND IMAGES AND COLOURS WORK TOGETHER

When you specify a background image (<BODY BACK-GROUND=" . . . . ">) also specify a background colour (<BODY BGCOLOR=" . . . . . ">). This should be similar to the main colour of any image on your page. If whoever is viewing your page has Autoload Image turned off, or if the background image can't load, the page will look much the same. If you are using another image on top of the background and that image has transparent areas (see Chapter 6 for information on images), remember that the background colour will show through. You may not get the effect you intended. This is another reason why it is best to test your Web page thoroughly before going live with it.

The good news
What Netscape 3.0 does allow that earlier versions didn't is for text and images to load before the background. It loads after, behind the text, so document loading is not slowed down by waiting for the colour to fill. If Auto Load Images is off, background colour (like other images) will not be loaded. If the background image is not loaded and a BGCOLOR was not specified, then the foreground colour attributes (LINK, VLINK and ALINK) will be ignored. This is a good thing, since your chosen text colours (grey, for example) might not show up at all on the default grey or white background. And who needs an apparently empty Web page?

But not all browsers support backgrounds. If you are using a graphical browser that supports HTML 3.0 you can change the background by including a GIF image. It is also possible to change the colour of the text. Among those browsers in which this is possible are Netscape 1.1 and higher, Microsoft Internet Explorer 2.0 and higher, and Mosaic for Microsoft Windows 2.0.0 plus others.

USING NETSCAPE'S BACKGROUNDS

No decent graphics package? Not good at graphics? Can't be bothered? Fortunately, the good people at Netscape have provided a set of graphics backgrounds that you can either:

- copy to the right directory on your hard disk *or*

- add as a hyperlink to your own HTML page so that they can be downloaded from the Netscape site when your page is on-line.

There are advantages and disadvantages to both of these methods.

Viewing and downloading the backgrounds
The backgrounds are a series of .gif files on a single Web page. They are at: *http://home.netscape.com/assist/net_sites/bg/backgrounds.html*

- Once in this page, right-click on the graphic of your choice and left-click on Save Image as... Wait until each graphic has fully displayed before right-clicking.

- Choose your directory – an /images subdirectory of your Web page directory would be a good place.

Advantage
The advantage of having these on your hard disk is that you can play around with them.

Disadvantage
They can take up quite a lot of disk space.

Using the backgrounds direct from the Netscape Web site
To refer to the backgrounds in your Web page, whether you have downloaded them or not, include a link as follows:

```
<BODY BACKGROUND="/assist/net_sites/bg/fabric/
gray_fabric.gif">
```

The URL for each of the backgrounds is shown with the image.

Advantage
The advantage of using the backgrounds directly from Netscape's server is that a user visiting a page on your site that uses a Netscape background may well have visited a page using the same background and it will be in the user's own \netscape\cache directory and load faster.

The majority of these images have about 30 colours in them, but they are stored as 256 colour images. This is a maximum. They are also 87a non-interlaced GIFs. You may want to change the format to transparent (89a) and interlaced, but that's up to you. See Chapter 6 for more information on GIF formats.

Disadvantage
It may take extra time to connect to the Netscape site and therefore slow up the first transfer of an image.

Creating a background image with tiling
You will have noticed that the background GIFs available from Netscape are quite small. So how do they fill a page? They are tiled – repeated horizontally and vertically. A background image will always be tiled. To put a colour pattern on your background, do this:
Create a yellow image 640 pixels wide and 10 pixels high (so viewers

won't see the tiling horizontally) and save it as yellow10.gif. The file size will be very small because it's only a few pixels high.

- Put this somewhere into a new HTML document with Notepad:
  `<IMG SRC="yellow10.gif">` (or use Insert Image)

- Save this file and view it in your browser.

- What you will see is a single bar of colour wherever you placed it in the document. Not what we wanted at all.

Now try this:

- Open a new HTML document.

- Type in this line using Notepad:
  `<BODY BACKGROUND="yellow10.gif">` or use Properties Document Appearance Background)

- Save this and view it in your browser. It will give you a seamless page of solid colour. But it was only 10 pixels high – so how does it fill a whole Web page? It was tiled.

GETTING CLEVER WITH BACKGROUND IMAGE TILING

You can now create some GIFs varying in a gradient. The example in Figure 9 used Paint Shop Pro, but it doesn't matter which graphics package you use so long as it can save in GIF format. These will be loaded one after the other to build a composite image on the page.

1. Create four GIFs that are each 640 x 10 but with a gradient in one colour, so they would look like the illustration (the example uses blue on a yellow background).

2. Save each of these in your images subdirectory.

3. Create a new HTML document and type into it:
   ```
   <BODY BGCOLOR="#FFFF90">
   <IMG SRC="gradedy1.gif"></CLEAR=LEFT>
   <IMG SRC="gradedy2.gif"></CLEAR=LEFT>
   <IMG SRC="gradedy3.gif"></CLEAR=LEFT>
   <IMG SRC="gradedy4.gif"></CLEAR=LEFT>
   ```

4. Save this document and view it in your browser. It will give you a page of solid colour with graded colour at the top, but all separated. Not the effect we're after.

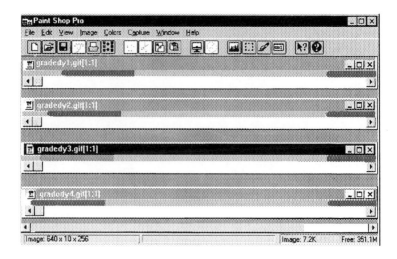

Fig. 9. Four GIF images varying in a gradient.

5.   Go back to your HTML document and add a line break to separate the four GIF image descriptions (in other words, the saved document will look like this):

```
<BODY BGCOLOR="#FFFF90">
<IMG SRC="gradedy1.gif"><BR CLEAR=LEFT>
<IMG SRC="gradedy2.gif"><BR CLEAR=LEFT>
<IMG SRC="gradedy3.gif"><BR CLEAR=LEFT>
<IMG SRC="gradedy4.gif"><BR CLEAR=LEFT>
```

6.   Remember to put the finished images and documents together in the c:/myweb directory you use for your Web pages. The /images subdirectory is just for development and to prevent confusion between different versions of the same file.

If you are having difficulty with seams and seamlessness, there is a Windows application that can help at *http://the-tech.mit.edu/KPT/ Makeback/makeback.html* This and other useful URLs are given at the end of this chapter.

CHANGING THE BACKGROUND COLOUR IN THE MIDDLE OF AN HTML DOCUMENT

This is not possible for most of us. Some browsers use style sheets, in which case it is possible. If you are using Netscape's Atlas navigator it is also possible. But let's stick to the real world and assume you have Netscape 3.0. These colour controls are attributes of the <BODY....> tag which you only set once for the whole document. Therefore you can't change colouring within a document. But you could specify a series of GIFs, loaded one after the other, or before and after text. Here is an example to try, although it looks rather garish when viewed.

1. Create eight GIFs in your graphics package with the filenames given in the lines below. Each GIF should be 640 x 50 and contain only the solid colour of the file name (red1.gif is solid red, for instance). Note that one is grey, and this will be your background.

2. Type the following lines into a new HTML document, rainbow.htm:

```
<HTML>
 <BODY BACKGROUND="GREY.GIF">
 <CENTER><TITLE> ALL THE COLOURS OF THE RAIN
 BOW</TITLE></CENTER>
 <IMG SRC="red1.gif">
 <CENTER>ALL</CENTER>
 <IMG SRC="orange1.gif">
 <CENTER>THE</CENTER>
 <IMG SRC="yellow1.gif">
 <CENTER>COLOURS</CENTER>
 <IMG SRC="green1.gif">
 <CENTER>OF</CENTER>
 <IMG SRC="blue1.gif">
 <CENTRE>THE</CENTER>
 <IMG SRC="indigo1.gif">
 <CENTER>RAINBOW</CENTER>
 <IMG SRC="violet1.gif">
 </BODY>
 </HTML>
```

3. Save, and view in your browser. Notice also that although you

specified the <BODY BACKGROUND . . .> colour only once, it was tiled so as to fill any part of the screen where there wasn't another GIF present.

CHANGING TEXT COLOUR IN AN HTML DOCUMENT

You can play around with the colour of text, too. Some browsers such as Netscape 2.0 and higher will support this. Change the text colour by adding a COLOR attribute to the FONT tag like this:

```
<FONT COLOR="#22AA00">Text</FONT>
```

This will print a piece of text in green. Use a HEX value as in <BODY BGCOLOR . . . >, <BODY TEXT . . . . >, etc. Look again at a slightly different version of the example given previously:

```
< HTML >
 <HEAD >
 <TITLE>Colour Example</TITLE>
 </HEAD>
 <BODY BGCOLOR="#000055" TEXT="#C0C0C0" LINK="
 #FF8000"ALINK="#3377FF"
VLINK= "#22AA00">
<P> In this example normal text is light-grey
(C0C0C00) on blue (000055), and <a href="terry1.
htm">hypertext</a> is yellow-orange (FFAA00),
</FONTCOLOR="#22AA00">green</FONT> (22AA00)
when activated, and </FONT COLOR="#3377FF">
light blue</FONT> (3377FF) if already visited.
</P>
 </BODY>
 </HTML>
```

Try adding this text at the end of rainbow.htm (before the <BODY tag, remember!). Each word (ALL, THE etc) is surrounded by a <FONT COLOR="#XXXXXX">. . . . .</FONT> statement. You can work out the HEX colour values to use, or try the following in turn:

```
<FONT COLOR="#FFFFFF">ALL</FONT>
<FONT COLOR="#FF00FF">THE</FONT>
<FONT COLOR="#FF9900">COLOURS</FONT>
<FONT COLOR="#FFFF00">OF</FONT>
<FONT COLOR="#00FF00">THE</FONT>
<FONT COLOR="#0000FF">RAINBOW</FONT>
<FONT COLOR="#0066CC">AT</FONT>
<FONT COLOR="#9900CC">ONCE</FONT>
```

LOSING THE

All through this chapter we have described colour values in the form #RRGGBB. Some browsers will accept the numbers alone without the hash sign (#), for example:

```
<FONT COLOR="00FF00">.
```

Try it, by all means, but this may not work with every browser. It is best to keep the hash.

ADDING TEXTURES

Your background image file needn't be a solid colour. It could be a texture such as weave, marble or paper. Paint Shop Pro comes with some texture gif files and others are available from Web sites listed below.

FINDING OUT MORE ABOUT COLOURS

There are many good sources of colours and information on colours. Try the following:

http://the-tech.mit.edu/KPT/Makeback/makeback.html
http://www.sci.kun.nl/thalia/guide/color
http://www.webmotion.com/Websurfshop/Colorcode
hhtp://catless.ncl.ac.uk/Lindsay/colours.html
http//colors.infi.net/colorindex.html

FINDING OUT MORE ABOUT TEXTURES

For more downloadable textures, try these Web sites

http://www.csv.warwick.ac.uk/~csuoq/window_managers/tiles/
*http://www.ecn.bgu.edu/users/gas52rO/Jay/Backgrounds/Back
grounds.html*
http://www.sausage.com/download/dl.reptile.html

6
Adding Images and Pictures

GETTING YOUR WEB PAGE NOTICED

Images are the most noticeable things on a Web page. It is possible to use interlaced GIF images which 'fade in' and a particular high-low resolution attribute where one image is loaded over another. There is also the possibility of animations and image maps containing clickable 'hot spots' that are links to another location.

Backgrounds and background colours
These are described in Chapter 5. Above all, make sure that your background and any images are compatible and do not clash.

CHOOSING GRAPHICS

If you want a really snazzy, zappy, image-filled Web page, go ahead. The problem is that a lot of browsers won't read the images or they'll take an age to load. An alternative is no graphics at all. But plain text is boring. So there's a happy medium – choose the right graphics and use them the right way.

Get a graphics package
First you have to create your graphics and for that you'll need a proper graphics package. There are hundreds out there from brain-dead articles like Paintbrush (don't bother, it can't handle GIF or JPEG) to industry-standard monsters like Corel. A lot of them are shareware so you can try them out. This chapter assumes you have or can get Paint Shop Pro, as described in Chapter 2. Others are listed at the end of this chapter.

Paint Shop Pro
One of the best graphics programs is JASC's Paint Shop Pro – it handles over 30 file formats and is one of the few shareware

programs actually worth paying for rather than uninstalling at the end of the trial period. So they get a free plug, but do tell them where you heard of it. Paint Shop Pro V3.12 in 16-bit (Windows 3.1 or 3.11) or 32-bit (Windows 95) is downloadable as shareware from: *http://www.digitalworkshop.co.uk/psp.htm* or it can be bought from

Digital Workshop, 19 Parsons Street, Banbury, Oxon OX16 8LY England. Tel: (01295) 258335. Fax: (01295) 254590.

Paint Shop Pro is one of the most commonly found programs on PC magazine CD-ROMs.

Helper Applications

Your browser handles graphics in two ways – either it reads them directly as in-line graphics (see below) or it uses a Helper Application (basically, it piggybacks on another program to display graphics). For instance, you may want to view 3-D molecular graphics and Netscape doesn't handle them. But there is a downloadable helper App called RasMol (and a few others) that can.

In-line graphics

More typically your browser will use in-line graphics handling which means the image is displayed as part of the Web page's layout, just as you intended. This only works for GIF and JPEG and not all flavours of those. But that's enough for our purposes just now.

Understanding GIF and JPEG compression formats

GIF (developed for CompuServe) and JPEG (the format determined by the Joint Photographic Experts Group) both compress graphics so that they download faster but in JPEG you can control the compression. The higher the compression, the smaller the downloaded file and the faster the download, but the price you pay is poorer quality – it's a balancing act. Moreover, GIF supports up to 256 colours (8 bits per pixel) and is therefore better for line art while JPEG can handle up to 16.7 million colours (24-bit) which is photographic quality and better than your monitor can actually display in all likelihood. But you can store both formats in fewer than the maximum number of colours and in greyscale.

GIF

GIF comes in a variety of versions – 87a and 89a – and both can be interlaced (see below) or non-interlaced. The differences are:

• 87a can't handle transparent GIFs.

• 89a can handle transparent GIFs – no annoying backgrounds which conflict with your lovingly chosen or multiple-image GIFs which you need for animations.

• Paint Shop Pro and GIF Construction Set (and other graphics packages) allow you to set transparency information – the image background doesn't appear when the picture is put into a Web page and the chosen page background shines through.

Interlacing
Interlacing means that the file downloads rather like a set of window blinds, becoming more and more defined as time rolls on, rather than loading from the top down. The advantage is that you get a good idea what the picture looks like before it has loaded completely, so you can decide whether to wait or move on.

BITS AND PIXELS

Your computer thinks in bits (**binary digits**) and your screen is composed of pixels (short for picture elements).

• **The bit** is the smallest unit of information on a computer. A single bit can be only 0 or 1. More meaningful information is obtained by combining consecutive bits – a byte is composed of 8 bits. Graphics are often described by the number of bits used to represent each dot. A 1-bit image is monochrome (0 or 1 = black or white) whereas an 8-bit image supports 256 (2^8) colours or shades of grey and 24- or 32-bit graphic is 'true' colour.

• **A pixel** is a single point in a graphic image. Graphics monitors display pictures by dividing the display screen into thousands or millions of pixels in rows and columns so close together that they appear as a colour image. On colour monitors, each pixel is composed of three dots – red, blue and green. Ideally, all three dots converge at the same point. The number of bits used to represent each pixel determines the number of colours or shades of grey which can be displayed – an 8-bit colour monitor can show 256 (2^8) colours or shades of grey.

The quality of a display monitor largely depends on its resolution, how many pixels it can display, and how many bits are used to represent each pixel. VGA monitors display 640 by 480 pixels (about 300,000), SVGA monitors display 1,024 by 768 (nearly 800,000) pixels and a True Colour monitor uses 24 bits per pixel, allowing more than 16 million colours.

The screen size and file size of a graphics file determine its download speed. The standard VGA screen size is 640 x 480 pixels and images should be kept as small as possible and *never* bigger than this, even if you are designing for a screen 800 x 600, as certain browsers will crash when presented with a larger image. The file size depends on how complex the image is and the resolution – how many colours it has.

Bitmaps and colours

Your graphics package may work in bitmaps or vector graphics. Bitmaps are like a grainy photograph, with each pixel described individually by a number of bits which describe the colour. Just as film speed determines how sharp the photograph is, the more bits per pixel the better the resolution. This ranges from 1 bit per pixel (either on or off) for black and white to 32 bits per pixel for over a billion colours, should you ever want them. Table 2 summarises bits and colours:

Table 2. Bits and colours.

Bits per pixel	Maximum colours	Why?	
1	2		2^1
4	16		2^4
8	256		2^8
15 or 16	32,768 (32K) or 65,536 (64K)	– depends on the format	2^{16}
24	16,777,216	– 'true' colour	2^{24}
32	1 billion-plus		2^{32}

Don't get confused between 32K colours (16-bit) and 32-bit colours (which require a 32-bit PC and software, such as Windows 95).

Your graphics package may produce files in vector graphics – the images are described by a series of mathematical formulae – but to use them in Web pages they will need to be converted to a bitmap format, GIF or JPEG.

Size is important

You can reduce a file's size by decreasing the number of colours used. Does your nifty little NEXT button need to be in 16.7 million colours? Possibly not. In fact 16 colour or 256 colour is more than adequate for most in-line image purposes. If someone really wants to download a superb photograph, they will put up with the slower download times for a 16 million-colour JPEG image, but don't put such things into your Web pages as in-line images. If someone wants to download an image from your Web page and blow it up without losing resolution the answer is to give them an option – put the small, low-colour version in your Web page (as a 'thumbnail') and hyperlink it to a downloadable version of the full-size, full-colour image on another page.

Table 3. Image file sizes.

Colours	Bits	Image size (pixels)			Comments
		160 x 120	320 x 240	640 x 480	
2	1	5 KB	20 KB	75 KB	Grainy B&W
16	4	20 KB	75 KB	300 KB	Looks horrid
256	8	40 KB	150 KB	600 KB	Can't tell the
32/64K	15/16	90 KB	300 KB	900 KB	difference
16.7 million	24	113 KB	450 KB	1.7 MB	between any of these

Just to show what this means, Table 3 gives the file sizes of the same image, a colour photograph, in GIF format at different screen sizes and colour resolutions. In other words, a 160 x 120 256-colour image is one-fortieth of the file size of the 640 x 480 24-bit version and will download correspondingly faster. Use your graphics package to generate various sizes, resolutions and number of colours until you find one you are happy with and which will not take up a vast amount of space. This is especially important if you are using free Web space on a server which only allows you 1MB or less total. One decent photograph will use up your entire allocation.

ADDING IMAGES IN NETSCAPE

Adding a picture in Netscape couldn't be easier.

1. Make sure the image file is in your directory, or a subdirectory of it (e.g. c:\myweb\image.gif or c:\myweb\pix\image.gif).

2. Use Insert Image to call up the dialogue box in Netscape Editor.

3. Type in the image file name, or use Browse to find it.

4. Give an alternative image if you want. A common trick is to have low-resolution of black and white image as an alternative which will load faster and let the viewer see what's coming.

5. Add some text to the Text box.

6. Save your file and view it in the browser.

You should now try the effects of the various alternatives in Alignment, Dimensions and Space to see what difference they make. Your image may, for instance, look better with a solid border around it. Or you may want it aligned with any associated text in a certain way.

Now you should look at the HTML source code to see what the code looks like.

USING THE IMAGE (IMG) TAG

< IMG SRC = "...". > - IMG tells the browser to look for an image. The attribute SRC gives the location of the image and is essential. There is no closing tag for <IMG>. Inside the quotes is the filename with the path and the file extension must be .gif or .jpg depending on whether the image is a GIF or a JPEG format.

The IMAGE tag is basically:

```
<IMG SRC="image.gif"> or < IMG SRC="image.jpg">
```

but it can have other attributes, including these:

```
IMG  SRC="image.gif"  ALIGN="LEFT/RIGHT/TOP/
TEXTTOP/MIDDLE/ABSMIDDLE/BASELINE/BOTTOM/ABS-
```

BOTTOM">

This positions the image and also tells the browser the relative positions of the graphic and any text appearing in the same line. Some browsers, like Netscape, display the in-line graphic and any text lines as you position them with ALIGN but others always show the text aligned with the bottom of the image. That's why it is essential to test the page in another browser before going 'live'.

- ALIGN = LEFT aligns the image at the next available space in the left margin and any following text will wrap around the right of the image.

- ALIGN = RIGHT aligns the image at the right margin, with the text wrapping to the left.

- ALIGN = TOP aligns the image with the top of the highest item in the line.

- ALIGN = TEXTTOP aligns the image with the top of the tallest text in the line (not always the same as ALIGN = TOP).

- ALIGN = MIDDLE aligns the middle of the image with the baseline of the line.

- ALIGN = ABSMIDDLE aligns the middle of the current line with the middle of the image.

- ALIGN = BASELINE aligns the bottom of the image with the baseline of the line.

- ALIGN = BOTTOM aligns the bottom of the image with the baseline of the line.

- ALIGN = ABSBOTTOM aligns the bottom of the image with the bottom of the line.

<IMG SRC="image 1.gif" ALT="Alternative text">
Always use ALT. This puts in a text message which displays if, for any reason, the file image1.gif can't be shown. This could be because:

- the image is corrupted or unavailable

- the viewer has turned off the browser's Option Autoload Images

- the viewer is using a non-graphical browser like Lynx.

Internet Explorer also uses any ALT text as a ToolTip displayed in a little box when the mouse is over the image.

`<IMG BORDER=value>`
This sets the width of the border around an image and can be set to 0 so that if the image is surrounded by `<A>`...`</A>` tags, the normal link border will not be shown.

`<IMG WIDTH=value HEIGHT=value>`
Use these to absolutely specify the space taken up by your image. If WIDTH and HEIGHT are used, the viewer of their document will not have to wait for the image to be loaded and its size calculated. The browser knows the layout of the text around the image and displays the text first and faster. WIDTH = "..." defines the size of the image. You could include HEIGHT = "..." in this `<IMG . . .>` line as well to absolutely define the size of image. If you leave it out the browser will resize your original image in proportion to the WIDTH = "..." value, maintaining the aspect ratio. If both are specified then the image is displayed accordingly. If it is stored on your disk as 120 x 240 and you specify width = "100" it will display as 100 x 200. If you specify width = "100" height = "100" it will appear that size, and squashed.

`<IMG VSPACE=value HSPACE=value>`
VSPACE and HSPACE control vertical space above and below the image and horizontal space to the left and right of the image. This sets a margin around the image which is useful to prevent text moving too close to images or images too close to each other. VSPACE = 0 and HSPACE = 0 are useful for making sure images *do* touch if you want them to.

`<IMG LOWSRC>`
It is possible to have two images in the same space. The command:

```
<IMG SRC="highres.jpg" LOWSRC="lowres.gif">
```

tells Netscape to load "lowres.gif" on its first pass. When the document and all its images are fully loaded, a second pass will load another image called "highres .jpg" in the same place. The low-resolution version will load quickly but a higher-resolution version can 'fade in' and replace it. Both images will be scaled by WIDTH = "..." and HEIGHT"..." attribute values if present. If the two images are of different sizes and WIDTH and HEIGHT not specified by IMG the image specified by the SRC attribute will be scaled to the size of the LOWSRC = "..." image.

Browsers that do not recognise the LOWSRC attribute simply load the image called "highres.gif" from the SRC = "..." command. This is an alternative to specifying another image using ALT, as described above.

  and CLEAR
Normally < BR > inserts a line break.

<BR CLEAR=LEFT> will break the line and move down until there is a clear left margin.
<BR CLEAR=RIGHT> is the same but for the right margin.
<BR CLEAR=ALL> moves down until both margins are free of images.

This is extremely useful for getting a series of images in a sequence.

Server-side image maps
< IMG ISMAP >
This tells the browser that the image as an image map – a graphic with clickable 'hot spots'. These clickable areas are linked ('mapped') to URLs. By clicking on different areas of the image, different links can be accessed, e.g.

```
<A  HREF="http://www.fifeweb.net/BDurie/
heraldry.htm">
<IMG SRC="shield.gif" ISMAP></A>
```

This make an entire image a clickable link and tells the browser that clicking on it will take the viewer to different parts of heraldry.htm. However, to use image maps in HTML documents, the HTTP server where the Web page resides must have the correct image map handling script installed to control the image map and define the 'hot-spots'.

Client-side image maps
There is an easier way – client-side image maps. Client-side image maps are invoked with a similar construction but using the USEMAP attribute instead, and providing the coordinates of hotspots with the <map> element:

```
<IMG SRC ="pic.gif" ALT="This is an image map"
USEMAP=" Info">
```

```
<MAP NAME="info">
<AREA NAME="circle" coords="20,30,..."
HREF="url.htm"<
</MAP>
```

This defines a circular area on the image of a certain size which, when clicked on, will send the browser to another document called url.htm. Area names rect (for rectangle) and polygon are also used. The length of the coords value must be fewer than 1,024 characters.

The image of a house (shown in Figure 10) called oldhouse.gif was converted into a client-side image map by adding coordinate data within a MAP statement. In this example clicking on each window would take the user to a different HTML document called 'window.htm'; clicking on the door would bring up 'door.htm'; clicking on the polygon surrounding the roof would activate 'roof.htm'; and there is a circular area within the door which would open 'knock.htm'. None of these documents exist but they would need to be written for the image map to be useful. They might contain information on insulation methods, for instance.

The tags and statements controlling this client-side image map will look something like this:

```
<HTML>
<BODY >
<IMG SRC="oldhouse.gif" USEMAP="#oldhouse">
<MAP NAME="oldhouse">
<AREA SHAPE=RECT COORDS="17,50,71,116"
HREF="window.htm">
<AREA SHAPE=RECT COORDS="82,52,130,116"
HREF="window.htm">
<AREA SHAPE=RECT COORDS="16,154,58,216"
HREF="window.htm">
<AREA SHAPE=RECT COORDS="91,154,133,213"
HREF="window.htm">
<AREA SHAPE=CIRCLE COORDS="72,168,13"
HREF="knock.htm">
<AREA SHAPE=RECT COORDS="50,145,96,233"
HREF="door.htm">
```

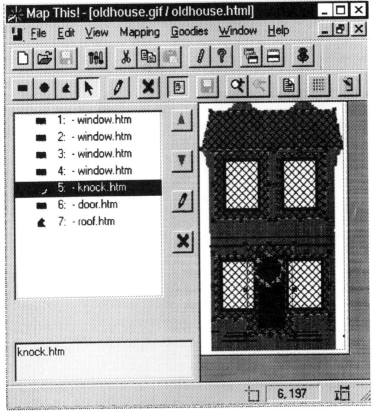

Fig. 10. The original GIF file (top) with the map overlays in
MapThis (bottom).

83

```
<AREA SHAPE=POLY COORDS="12,8,2,46,148,46,141,8,12,8"
HREF="roof.htm">
</MAP>
</BODY>
</HTML>
```

Line by line
```
<IMG SRC="oldhouse.gif" USEMAP="#oldhouse">
```

This tells the browser the name of the image file and that it is a client-side image map. It also defines the bookmark (#oldhouse) where the MAP information resides, later in the document.

```
<MAP NAME="oldhouse">
```
This is the bookmark, after which the MAP information starts.

```
<AREA SHAPE=RECT COORDS="17,50,71,116"
HREF="window.htm">
```
This defines a clickable AREA. The SHAPE is a rectangle whose opposite corners are the coordinates shown. Clicking takes the browser to window.htm

The other AREA lines define other rectangles, a circle (with the centre coordinate and radius shown) and a polygon (all defining points listed). Notice that the line for 'knock.htm' appears before that for 'door.htm' so the knock circle is 'on top' of the door rectangle.

```
</MAP>
```
This closes the mapping information and is enclosed within the BODY of the document.

Working out the coordinates
How do you work out what the coordinates are? There are three ways.

1. Print your chosen image to scale on graph paper and work it out. Laborious, very.

2. If your graphics package has a cursor counter, move the cursor to a chosen spot and write down the coordinates. Not much better.

3. Download a wonderful freeware program called MapThis from
    Todd C. Wilson/Fresh Ground Software at *http://gale-
    driel.ecaetc.ohio-state.edu/tc/mt* This program will do it all for
    you, not without some careful reading of the Help file, but
    competently. Figure 10 shows the MapThis screen and how it
    looks after the Area maps have been added.

You can now include clickable image maps in your Web pages.

Captions

To include text with an image like a caption put the <IMG
SRC="picture.gif"> tag immediately before the text. Try
putting both of the lines below into an HTML document – choose
your own picture and make sure it's in the same directory as your
HTML document. Alter the text to suit the image. Make sure the
picture is 120 pixels wide (resize it with your graphics package).
Save, then look at the results in your browser with AutoLoad
Images turned on, then off.:

<IMG SRC="image.gif"> This is my favourite picture. It is
called 'image.gif'.
<IMG ALIGN=BOTTOM SRC="vitbsmal.gif" ALT="No
picture available" width=100> This is my favourite
picture. It is called 'image.gif'.

Notice the use of the single quote – see Special Characters in Chapter 4.

USING IMAGES AS LINKS

You can use an in-line image as a way of getting to a hyperlink, as in
the myfile.htm exercise earlier in the book. Clicking on the image
will take the browser to another part of the document, to another
document or to another URL elsewhere. This can be achieved by
selecting the image in the HTML document, clicking on the link
button and filling in the information in the dialogue box.
Alternatively, you could type in a command line such as:

<A HREF="another.html"><IMG SRC="pie.gif"></A>

where the <IMG....> command is whatever you had before – in
other words, you surround the picture command line with <A
HREF...> and </A>. You will see a difference when you browse

your saved file – the graphic with a hypertext link has a border around it. Take this out, if you want, with the BORDER=X tag where X is the width of the border in pixels. BORDER=0 means no border, or rather, a border of zero width.

Nice image if you can get it

To see a good example of how to use a much sought-after graphic image in an interesting way, look at Pamela Anderson in *http://www.norr.mm.se/HEMLIS/HEMLIS.html*. It won't offend, promise.

Three things to remember

1. Be careful with images
Because images are so freely available on The Web, there is a temptation to use, copy, alter and redistribute them like confetti. Be aware that most images belong to someone and it is not only impolite, it is hazardous to your legal health to treat them as your own.

2. Watch the addressing
There is a glitch in Netscape Editor which will sometimes retain the absolute address of a graphic added using Insert Image Browse. This means that if your graphic was in a directory called c:\windows and you used Browse to copy it to your directory it may appear as something like *file:///C|/myweb/image.gif* which will be meaningless to the server once you upload your page for public consumption. This can also happen if you cut and paste a graphic from one part of your web page to another. The only reliable way to deal with this is to edit the document source and take out everything before the graphic's file name. Yes, in every web document. In practice this bit of housework is the very last thing to do after constructing a web site – open every HTML document in Notepad, check for absolute addresses and take them out. Be careful not to accidentally remove any other code or tags, especially < or > which can be a nightmare to put right later. Not a job for the early hours of the morning.

3. Have fun
Well, why bother with images otherwise?

EXPLORING OTHER GRAPHICS PACKAGES

You might like to try these:

- DTA (Dave's Targa Animator)
  http://www.europa.com/~dearmad/dta.htm
  This will handle GIF, TIF, PCX and BMP (all you need, really, except JPEG) and can take sequential GIFs and turn them into an Autodesk Animator sequence.

- GifCon (GIF Construction Set)
  http://www.mindworkshop.com/alchemy/gifcon.html
  This is useful for making transparent GIFs and animated GIFs, more of which later. It can also be downloaded from a mirror site (another server closer to you). The alchemy page will direct you.

- Photo Studio
  It's not a patch on Paint Shop Pro but it's widely available on the cover disks of magazines and is worth a look.

7
Putting Tables in Your Web Pages

CREATING SIMPLE TABLES

Tables are just about the only way to lay out a document as you would like to. They give you a degree of control over size and positioning of text and graphics not really possible any other way. Tables are extremely useful – the top row and left-hand column can explain what the rows below them and the columns beside them contain. They are a great method for presenting information succinctly and in an easy-to-read form. In the bad old days, before HTML was up to tables, the only way to do it was with pre-formatted text, fixed-width columns and the like. Now life is simpler – HTML tags can do it all.

Using Netscape Editor
As usual, Netscape Editor makes the task fairly straightforward, although you do have to know how many rows and columns you want as it can be tricky to add them afterwards. Try creating a 2 x 2 table with a different colour background in each:

1.   Insert Table with 2 rows and 2 columns.

2.   Use Properties Table to change the attributes of each cell such as background colour, relative size, etc.

3.   Add text into the table cells afterwards.

Notice (see Figure 11) what happens if you specify or do not specify the Cell Width – long text will 'stretch' the cell unless you specify its width in either pixels or percentage of the screen size.

Using HTML
Type these lines below into an HTML document in Notepad, save and view it with Netscape.

Table 1

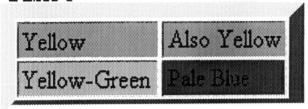

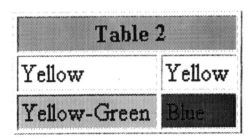

Fig. 11. Two different table results.

```
<TABLE BORDER=10>
<TH> Table 1</TH>
<TR BGCOLOR="#FFFF00">
<TD> Yellow </TD>
<TD> Also Yellow </TD>
</TR>
<TR>
<TD BGCOLOR="#DDFF55"> Yellow-Green </TD>
<TD BGCOLOR="#8888EE"> Pale Blue </TD>
</TR>
</TABLE></P>
<TABLE BORDER>
<TR BGCOLOR="#FFFF00">
<TH COLSPAN=2> Table 2</TH>
</TR>
<TR>
<TD> Yellow </TD>
```

```
<TD> Yellow </TD>
</TR>
<TR>
<TD BGCOLOR="#DDFF55"> Yellow-Green
</TD>
<TD BGCOLOR="#8888EE"> Blue
</TD>
</TR>
</TABLE>
```

You will notice a number of things in the illustration:

- There are two tables.

- The tables contained cells of different colours which were defined with HEX codes, but colours might have done.

- Table 1 had a larger border, set by the <TABLE BORDER=10> tag.

- Yellow was only specified once, so it was retained for the second table cell.

- Table 1 was 2 x 2 cells, Table 2 was different. This is because, in Table 1, there were two <TD>...</TD> tags within <TR>...</TR> tags – so there are two Table Data cells in this Table Row.

- In Table 2 the description 'Table 2' was inside a cell, because the <TH>Table2</TH> header command came after the <TABLE....> command. Notice also it was bold and centred (default) and across two columns (<TH COLSPAN=2> Table 2</TH>).

- The width of the cells adjusted according to the length of the text within them. Compare the first and second tables.

Writing a table in HTML
A set of table tags should look like this:

```
<TABLE BORDER=2>
```
Starts table (Border is optional)

```
<CAPTION> caption contents</CAPTION>
```
Optional

```
<TR>
```
Start of first row

```
<TH>Text</TH>
```
Text in first cell in row 1 (Head)

```
<TH>Text</TH>
```
Text in next cell in row 1 (Head)

```
</TR>
```
Closes first row (2 columns because 2 <TH>tags)

```
<TR>
```
Start of next row

```
<TD>Text</TD>
```
Text in first cell in row 2

```
<TD>Text</TD>
```
Text in next cell in row 2

```
</TR>
```
Closes second row

```
<TR>
```
Start of last row

```
<TD>Text</TD>
```
Text in first cell in row 3

```
<TD> Text</TD>
```
Text in first cell in row 3

```
</TR>
```
Closes last row

```
</TABLE>
```
Closes table

The number of <TR>...</TR> tags defines the number of rows. The number of <TD> ..</TD> or <TH>...</TH> tags within <TR>...</TR> specifies the number of cells (and therefore columns) within that row. Because each row is formatted independently there is considerable flexibility.

A table for tables

Just to make that point, Table 4 summarises what you need to know to do tables, and Table 5 gives the codes to produce a table like those in Figure 11.

Table 4. Table tags.

Table element	Description
`<TABLE>...</TABLE>`	This must enclose all the other table tags and should be within the `<BODY>...</BODY>` tags.
`<TH>...</TH>`	Table Header cell – unless you specify otherwise the text will be bold and centred. Table Header cells can contain Table Attributes (see below).
`<TR>...</TR>`	Table Row – used to define Attributes for each row such as `<TR> ALIGN (LEFT, CENTER, RIGHT)>Text</TR>`.
`<TD>...</TD>`	Table Data cell – text is aligned left and centred vertically by default. Other Attributes can be added. Each time it is used it refers to the next cell in turn.
`<CAPTION>...</CAPTION>`	Inserts a caption in the table. By default this is centred and at the top. Use `<CAPTION ALIGN=BOTTOM>` to put the caption below the table and any other Markup tag (`<B>...</B>` etc.).

Table 5. Table codes

Table attributes	Description
`ALIGN (LEFT, CENTER,RIGHT)`	Alignment of cell contents horizontally.
`BORDER=X`	Display the table with a border. X is the width of the border, in pixels.
`BGCOLOR="#RRGGBB"`	Give the table, row or cell a background colour.
`VALIGN (TOP, MIDDLE, BOTTOM)`	Alignment of cell contents vertically.
`COLSPAN=x`	The number (x) of columns spanned by a cell.
`ROWSPAN=y`	The number (y) of rows spanned by a cell.
`NOWRAP`	No word wrapping within a cell.
Notes:	Any Attributes in `<TH>...</TH>` or `<TD>...</TD>` cells override the defaults set in a `<TR>...</TR>`. You can also include background colour, text colour and other attributes, including hyperlinks with table cells.

CLICK ANYWHERE ON THE PICTURE
Tourist Information - Where to go next?

Fig. 12. Four clickable images looking like one, in a 2 x 2 table with zero
borders, spacing and padding.

EXPLORING THE FLEXIBILITY OF TABLES

Tables aren't just for tabular information. This makes them perfect
for other sorts of uses. Figure 12 is an example of four hyperlinks in
a table with no borders. As far as the viewer is concerned, this is one
image with four 'hot spots'. It was created by splitting one image
into four exactly the same size in a graphics package, saving each of
the quadrants separately and inserting one GIF and one hyperlink
per cell, each to a different URL (a GIF image of a map in the
images subdirectory). Try it – you should have a map like this in
your clipart with Windows.

1. Import it as a clipart picture into a Word document.

2. Mark the picture and save it as a .bmp file in your myweb
    directory.

3. This can be opened in Paint Shop Pro and resaved as a .gif file.

4. You can then cut the quarters out of it and store each in a different .gif file (here called nw1.gif, ne1.gif, etc.).

5. Use Notepad to construct a new HTML document with this text:

```
<HTML>
<TABLE BORDER=0 CELLSPACING=0 CELLPADDING=0>
<CAPTION> CLICK ANYWHERE ON THE PICTURE
<CAPTION>
<TR BGCOLOR=C0C0C0>
<TH COLSPAN=2> Tourist Information - Where to go
next? </TH>
</TR>
<TR>
<TD><A HREF="pages/nw1info.htm"><IMG BORDER=0
SRC="images/nw1.gif"></A></TD>
<TD><A HREF="pages/ne1info.htm"><IMG
BORDER=0 SRC="images/ne1.gif"></A></TD>
</TR>
<TR>
<TD><A HREF="pages/sw1info.htm"><IMG BORDER=0
SRC="images/sw1.gif"></A></TD>
<TD><A HREF="pages/se1info.htm"><IMG BORDER=0
SRC="images/se1.gif"l></A>
</TD>
</TR>
</TABLE>
/<HTML>
```

Really it is four individual GIFs (see Figure 13). The files that the hyperlinks point to (NW1info.htm, etc.) could be tourist information, climatic data, etc. The trick is to specify attributes such as CELLSPACING, CELLPADDING, BORDER all at =0 so there is no seam between rows or columns.

Incidentally, it is possible to save Excel spreadsheet tables as HTML. There are also various utilities available to create and

Fig. 13. The four individual GIFs which make up the single clickable image in Figure 12.

convert tables, including Internet Assistant for Excel.

Watching the borders
Because pictures as hyperlinks have borders by default, the attribute BORDER = 0 must be added to the < IMG . . .> tags. Images can also be placed within single cell tables with borders by leaving the BORDER attribute out or by giving it a value greater than 0.

Changing fonts within tables
When any <TABLE> element is encountered any previous <BASEFONT> or <FONT> definitions are ignored and the text reverts to the default text size (which is set in the viewer's browser preferences). This could get in the way of your beautiful layout.

However, <FONT> settings can be specified inside every cell of the
table using the FONT attribute after each <TD>. Try this in a new
HTML document (remembering the <HEAD> and <BODY> tags as
usual).

```
<BASEFONT SIZE= "6">Text size (6)
<TABLE BORDER=2>
  <TR>
    <TD><FONT SIZE="6" COLOR="RED">Font size 6,
    red</FONT></TD>
    <TD>Default text size (4) and colour</TD>
  </TR>
  <TR>
    <TD><FONT SIZE="-1" COLOR="BLUE">Default
    text size -1 (=3) blue</TD>
    <TD><FONT COLOR="BLUE">Default text size
    again<BR>Still blue</TD>
  </TR>
</TABLE>
```

This text is size 6, the base font outside the table. The <BASEFONT>
tag is set to 6, but none of the <TABLE> cells uses this. The cells
without a particular <FONT> setting display in the browser's default
text size and colour (taken from the preferences). After the table, the
document reverts to the <BASEFONT> values (see Figure 14). To set
a font size, colour or other attribute different from the default text,
use an explicit <FONT> setting after every <TD> tag.

Adding rows and columns
It always happens – you construct your table then discover you need
an extra row. The simple way to deal with this is as follows:

- In the example immediately above, edit the document source in
  Notepad.

- Go to just before the < TABLE > tag.

- Type in <TR><TD></TD><TD></TD></TR> (assuming you
  have two columns in your table – if there are more, add extra </
  TD><TD>tags).

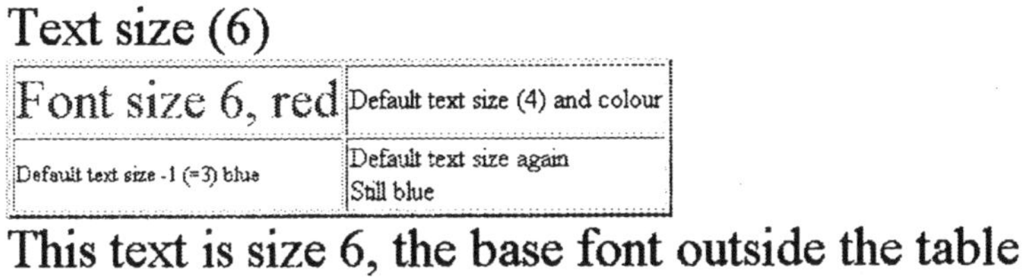

Text size (6)

Font size 6, red	Default text size (4) and colour
Default text size -1 (=3) blue	Default text size again Still blue

This text is size 6, the base font outside the table

Fig. 14. Changing fonts within a table.

- To add an extra column to the whole table, you will need to put an additional </TD><TD> before every </TR>.

- Save and view.

In Netscape Editor you can use the Insert Table command to add rows, columns, cells or whole tables (see below) within a table.

PUTTING TABLES WITHIN TABLES

A table cell can itself contain a table. The structure of a web page could be something like this:

```
<HTML>
  <HEAD><TITLE></TITLE></HEAD>
    <BODY>
      <TABLE BORDER=1 WIDTH="50%">
      <TR>
        <TD></TD>
        <TD></TD>
        <TD></TD>
      </TR>
      <TR>
        <TD></TD>
        <TD>
        <TABLE BORDER=1 WIDTH="80%">
        <TR>
        <TD></TD>
        <TD></TD>
```

```
      </TR>
      <TR>
       <TD></TD>
       <TD></TD>
      </TR>
      </TABLE>
      </TD>
      <TD></TD>
    </TR>
    <TR>
     <TD COLSPAN="3"></TD>
    </TR>
    </TABLE>
  </BODY>
</HTML>
```

The web page would look like Figure 15.

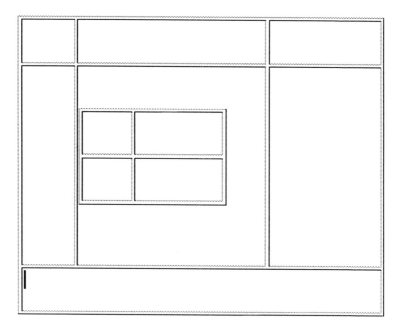

Fig. 15. A table within the cell of a table – note that the last row is one cell which spans three columns.

SUMMARY

- Tables allow you to absolutely specify where and at what size you would like to place:
  - text
  - graphics
  - links to other page components.

- You can have tables within tables.

8
Putting Forms in Your Web Pages

UNDERSTANDING WHAT A FORM DOES

Forms send information

Forms are a method of getting a viewer to send information to the Web server holding your Web site. The most common example is the 'I am over 18' tick box, the entry of credit card details or the collection of names and e-mail addresses. The form allows the information to be sent to you for some action, which could be a return e-mail (dealt with in a later chapter) or addition of the viewer's details to a database. The text and other elements you type into a form and the data from the buttons or checkboxes you click are collected by your browser and sent as a request to the server that holds the form HTML document. This accesses a program on the server or within another URL which is specified by an ACTION attribute in the form, as you will see.

The Common Gateway Interface (cgi)

Sometimes the ACTION is just sending an e-mail. But if the server has to handle the data in any way (put it into a database, for example, or send back information to you) it will have one or more programs called 'Common Gateway Interface' programs, or cgi scripts. These cgi programs are typically held in a server directory called cgi-bin, so they have come to be known as cgi-bin scripts. The cgi scripts and other processing programs are written in a programming language which can handle the information. Perl is a good example as are Pascal, C and even Basic, but such programming is outside the scope of this book. However, there are shareware and freeware off-the-shelf programs and scripts available on The Web to help you do this. Even without this, you can still construct forms and make sense of the information they send.

Getting information with forms

Forms are often used to get as well as send information. In fact, it was a desire to use The Web to access databases that led to the development of the Common Gateway Interface. When you use The Web to get to a library database, you are usually filling in a form presented to your browser in the HTML document you are reading and sending the request to a cgi-bin on some server.

Get your cgi here

One place to start is the NCSA (National Centre for Super-computing Applications). Their HTTPd is an HTTP/1.0 compatible server for making hypertext and other documents available to Web browsers. The URL is *http://hoohoo.ncsa.uiuc.edu/docs/Overview.html* but do read the copyright notice that accompanies it. Alternatively, get someone (a college student, for instance) to write the program for you.

CONSTRUCTING A SIMPLE FORM

Using the FORM tag

The <FORM...>...</FORM> tags are new additions to the Web creator's armoury to make them possible. Forms have the same general structures as the other HTML tags we have used so far.

Using INPUT and TEXTAREA fields

What you have to define within your form are the input fields. If you wanted to collect one line of information (the viewer's name, perhaps) you could use either INPUT or TEXTAREA. Try the following two examples in a single form to see the effect of different elements.

```
<HTML>
<HEAD><TITLE>TRYOUT</TITLE></HEAD>
Input and text area
  <BODY>
    <FORM>
      <INPUT name="yourname" type="text">Type
      your name here<BR>
    <P>
        <TEXTAREA name="yourname2" rows="1"
```

```
        cols="20">Type your name here.
        </TEXTAREA>
        </FORM>
     </BODY>
  </HTML>
```

The two tags <FORM>....</FORM> tell your browser that the HTML code between them is a form. <INPUT> defines a text entry area called "yourname" and the input type is "text". The text after the tag is an instruction which will appear on your web page. Note that <INPUT> has no closing tag.
 provides a line break. <P> starts a new paragraph and introduces a blank line. <TEXTAREA>...</TEXTAREA> specifies a text entry area called "yourname2" of a specific size (1 x 20) within which text will scroll. The instructional text is within the box. Try the following:

• Leave out the <BR> and/or <P> and see the difference in layout.

• Change the TEXTAREA tag attributes and values to:

```
<TEXTAREA name="yourname2" rows="2" cols="30">
```

• Move the instructional text out of the TEXTAREA tags:

```
<TEXTAREA name="yourname2" rows="1"
cols="20"></TEXTAREA>Type your name here.
```

CONSTRUCTING COMPLEX FORMS

Now construct a complex form, see it working and then examine the elements of it. Let's say you wanted to collect a few items of information – name, postcode, telephone number and e-mail address plus some preference details, for instance – for a cornflakes promotion. You set up a form that asks for input as follows:

```
     <HTML>
      </HEAD>
        <TITLE>CORNFLAKE COMPETITION </TITLE>
      </HEAD>
   <CENTER>CORNFLAKE COMPETITION</CENTER>
    <hr SIZE=5 WIDTH=25%>
```

```
<FORM method="POST" action="mailto: joe
soap.@flakes.com.ar">
  <p>Name: <input name="name" type="text"
  size="20">
  E-MAIL: <input e-mail="e-mail"type=
  "text" size="30"><br>
    Favourite colour: <select name=
    "favcolour">
    <option>Blue<option>Red<option>Green
    <option>Purple<option></select>
      <TEXTAREA  name="othercolour"
      rows="1" columns="12"></textarea>
      Another colour?
  </p>
  <p><textarea name="slogan" rows="3"
  columns="50">
Please write a slogan for our new cornflakes
here, in not more than 25 words...
    </TEXTAREA>
  </p>
  Please  help  us  by  answering  a  few
  questions about yourself
  <P>Your company's name <INPUT NAME="Co"
  TYPE=text SIZE="48">
  <P>Based  in  the  UK?  <INPUT NAME="UK?"
  TYPE=checkbox>
    How many employees? <INPUT NAME="emps"
    TYPE=int SIZE="6">
  <P>Which browsers do you use?
<OL>
 <LI>Netscape  2.0  <INPUT  NAME="browsers"
 TYPE=radio VALUE="NN2">
 <LI>Netscape  3.0  <INPUT  NAME="browsers"
 TYPE=radio VALUE="NN3">
 <LI>Lynx <INPUT NAME="browsers" TYPE=radio
 VALUE="Lynx">
```

```
    <LI>Another <INPUT NAME="other" SIZE=40>
    </OL>
Please give us a name for further contact: <INPUT
NAME="contact" SIZE="42">
Speak now <INPUT NAME="contact" TYPE=audio>
<p>Which are your three favourite breakfast
foods?
    <select name="breakfast" multiple>
      <option> corn flakes
      <option> ricicles
      <option> muesli
      <option> bran flakes
      <option> bacon & eggs
      <option> toast
      <option> three cigarettes
    </select></p>


    <p>(Option list) Hit return and use arrow keys
    and return to select option


    <p><input type="submit" value="GO"> <input
    type="reset"></p>
</form>
    <hr NOSHADE SIZE=10 WIDTH=75%>
```

When this form is filled in and sent as an e-mail message (by
pressing the Submit button now labelled GO) the receiver gets an e-
mail like the one below – the contents will depend on what you
typed in.

```
Content-type: application/x-www-form-urlencoded
Content-length: 273
name = John + Q + Public&e-mail = JQP@server.com&fav
colour = Blue&othercolour = Pink&slogan = THEY + ARE +
RUBBISH%21 + + + + + + + + + Please + write + a +
slogan + for + our + new + cornflakes + here%2C + in + not
+ more + than + 25 + words...%0D%0A + + + + + + + + +
&Co = The + Big + Company&UK%3F = on&emps = 1&
```

browsers = NN3&other = Spry&contact = me& contact = xxx& breakfast = three + cigarettes

You should play around with the various aspects of this form. Below are the details of the tags, attributes and values. Notice the use of an Ordered List with <OL>...</OL> and <LI> tags.

The FORM tag and attributes

● <FORM>...</FORM> tells the browser a form is contained within the tags. Attributes are ACTION, METHOD and ENCTYPE.

● <FORM METHOD="..." ACTION="url"> Text </FORM> is the instruction what to do with the information.

● The METHOD attribute is either GET for queries) or POST (for collection of data such as e-mail addresses) GET is the default method. The form contents are attached to your URL as if they were a normal query. POST, however, sends the form contents in a data packet. Using GET can overload the server if more than a few hundred bytes of data are submitted all at once. This is not a problem with POST. Use POST rather that GET whenever you can.

● ACTION in this case is mailto: and the value is your e-mail URL. In the script above, change: "mailto:joesoap@flakes. com.ar" to include your own e-mail address. The URL could otherwise be a reference to the script or program which handles the data.

● ENCTYPE tells the form to encode the form's contents for sending. You can ignore this because it only applies to METHOD = "POST" and there is only one value allowed at the moment (application/x-www-form-urlencoded). Forget about it.

Within the <FORM>...<?FORM> tags you can have INPUT, TEXTAREA and SELECT as the interactive elements.

The INPUT tag
The attributes of INPUT are these:

1. NAME is a term associated with an INPUT or SELECT field which will be meaningful when the data is processed. In the example above there is a text box with the label 'favourite colour' but the symbolic name we set for this is 'favcolour'.

NAME must be present for every TYPE (see below) except SUBMIT and RESET. All INPUT fields of a radio or checkbox group must have the same NAME.

2. The TYPE could be any one of these:

    - AUDIO

    - CHECKBOX (a single toggle box for non-exclusive choices; on or off, checked or empty)

    - FILE

    - HIDDEN (a text entry box which does not display the characters entered

    - PASSWORD (a text entry field but any characters entered are represented as asterisks)

    - RADIO (a single toggle button for exclusive choices; on or off, and checked or empty)

    - RESET (a push-button that clears the form – the name on the button can be changed with VALUE)

    - SCRIBBLE (a text entry box)

    - SUBMIT a push-button which sends the form data to the processing server – you can call this button by any name you like, as with reset)

    - TEXT (a text entry field – the default).

3. VALUE in a tag like BGCOLOR is easy to understand – it is the value of that colour. In a TEXT or PASSWORD entry, VALUE determines the default contents of the field – the data it will send (such as nothing at all) if you don't change it with an entry of some sort.

4. VALUE in a RADIO button or CHECKBOX determines the value of the button when it is checked. Be sure that you want the checked box or filled radio button to mean what you think it means when checked. Unchecked boxes and buttons send no data and are ignored but the default value is 'on' unless you change it. The difference between CHECKBOX and RADIO is that CHECKBOX is for non-exclusive choices – if there are more than one CHECKBOX items, some, all or none could be checked. RADIO is for exclusive choices (like YES or NO).

Checking any one unchecks all others. There is only one result sent.

5. VALUE for Submit and Reset can be used to change the text on the button – SUBMIT could be changed to GO or Send, RESET to Clear or anything else you find meaningful in your form.

6. CHECKED in checkboxes and radio buttons determines that the box or button is checked by default.

7. SIZE is the number of characters (also called columns) or rows of a text input field. If not present, the default is 20, which may be enough for a name, but perhaps not a street address or an e-mail address. Text entry fields that will occupy more than one line or row can be specified with SIZE = width,height as in SIZE = 40,4 (40 characters and four lines). Note that this is different from COLSPAN = in a table or WIDTH = for a line (< HR >) – these are in pixels. SIZE works in characters at the standard font size. However, it is better to use the TEXTAREA tag for text entry boxes more than one line high.

8. MAXLENGTH is the maximum number of characters that can be entered. This is especially useful for passwords but only applies to single-line text fields. The default is unlimited length. But even if the allowed text entry is (in theory) infinite, the text box will have scroll bars if MAXLENGTH is more than SIZE.

The SELECT and OPTION tags
SELECT has opening and closing tags, unlike INPUT. Within the SELECT tags you may only have a series of OPTION tags plus plain text (no HTML markup). SELECT can have these attributes:

• NAME: this *must* be present in SELECT.

• SIZE: if SIZE is 1 or if the SIZE attribute is missing (as in our examples) the box will reflect the length of the contents. If SIZE is 2 or more, SELECT will provide a scrolled list. The value determines how many items are visible. See over for two examples of this.

• MULTIPLE, if present but with no VALUE allows SELECT to present as many results as the viewer selects. In the above example, VALUE should have been set to 3, since we asked for the three favourite breakfasts. Try it. MULTIPLE also makes

SELECT a scrolled list, regardless of the SIZE.

<SELECT>...</SELECT> and <SELECT><OPTION>...</OPTION>...</SELECT> can be used to produce choice menus. Notice that we used this two different ways:

```
Favourite colour: <select name="favcolour">
<option>Blue<option>Red<option>Green<option>
Purple</select>
```

and:
```
<select name="breakfast" multiple>
  <option> corn flakes
  <option> ricicles
  <option> muesli
  <option> bran flakes
  <option> bacon & eggs
  <option> toast
  <option> three cigarettes
</select></p>
```

In this example, all the OPTION statements are in a single line so that it becomes a drop-down menu. The breakfast OPTION tags are in an ordered list so that all are visible. OPTION can have a VALUE which is either selected or disabled. If no value is given, the element text content is used. Putting SELECTED within an OPTION means that this option is always selected. If MULTIPLE is present then more than one (any in fact) of the options can be specified as SELECTED.

The TEXTAREA tags
The attributes to TEXTAREA are:

• NAME as with INPUT and SELECT.

• ROWS – the vertical height (in characters).

• COLS – horizontal width (in characters).

A TEXTAREA field, unlike an INPUT field, always has scrollbars but like an INPUT field it can have any amount of text entered into it.

A TEXTAREA box can have default content specified. In the first example in this chapter we first entered default content (instructional script), then removed it to outside the TEXTAREA box.

The contents must be straight text with no markup, but you can enter line breaks.

Multiple forms

Inside <FORM...</FORM> you can have as many SELECT tags as you wish along with INPUT, TEXTAREA and bits of readable text. But you cannot have forms within forms. You can, however, have more than one form in a document like this:

```
<HTML>
  <HEAD>
   <FORM>
     The form's contents
   </FORM>
     <FORM>
     The next form's contents
     </FORM>
  <HEAD>
<HTML>
```

Adding images

Images can, of course, be used to cheer up forms, as can BACKGROUND images and BGCOLOUR. You could put a picture of a cornflakes packet on the form with the line:

```
<IMG SRC="CORNFLAK.GIF">
```

If you had such an image.

CHECKLIST: FORM TAGS

The tags in HTML for forms are:

- <FORM>...</FORM> Surrounds a form. Attributes are ACTION, METHOD, ENCTYPE.

- <INPUT> Defines an input field. Attributes are NAME, TYPE, VALUE, CHECKED, SIZE, MAXLENGTH.

- <SELECT>...</SELECT> Surrounds a selection list. Attributes are NAME, MULTIPLE, SIZE.

- <OPTION> Specifies a selection (within a SELECT). Attribute is SELECTED.

- <TEXTAREA>...</TEXTAREA> Defines a text input field. Attributes are NAME, ROWS, COLS.

TESTING YOUR FORM

1. Test the layout locally

Save your form as a .htm file and load it into your browser off-line (i.e. your browser program is open but you are not connected to a server). You can have your text editor or HTML editor open at the same time and make changes to this, saving and reloading to the browser as you go. Note that you may have to use File Open File in Browser as Reload may just take the last version from the cache and not reflect all the changes.

2. Send it to yourself

Put your own e-mail address in the ACTION = "mailto:*your e-mail address*" and check your mail later. There is an example of this above. Notice that filed returns are separated by '&' and individual words within them by + signs.

3. Test the layout for real

NCSA has a query server that will return to you what you submitted with name/value pairs decoded and itemised. Use one or both (separately) of the following:

```
<METHOD="POST" ACTION="http://hoohoo.
ncsa.uiuc.edu/cgi-bin/post-query"
```

or

```
METHOD= "GET" ACTION= "http://hoohoo.
ncsa.uiuc.edu/cgi-bin/query"
```

TRYING OUT SOME SAMPLE FORMS

Here are some samples you can try out. Remember to enclose all

HTML text within <HTML>...</HTML> and include < HEAD > < TITLE >.... < /TITLE > < /HEAD > tags with each one.

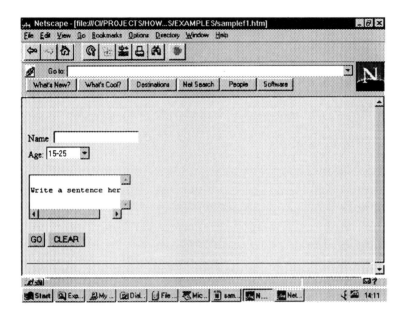

Fig. 16. Sample form 1.

Sample form 1 (Figure 16)

```
<HTML >
<HEAD><TITLE>Sample form 1</TITLE></HEAD>
<BODY bgcolor="lightblue">
   <hr size=2 width=100%>
     <FORM method="GET" action="http://hoohoo.
     ncsa.uiuc.edu/cgi-bin/query">
       <p>Name:<input  name="response_name"
       type="text" size="20"><br>
         Age: < select name="response_age">
         <option>15-25<option>26-35<option
         >36-45<option>46-55<option>56-65
         <option>Over 65<option></select></p>
       <p>textarea name="comments "rows="3"
```

```
        columns="40">
Write a sentence here...</textarea></p>
        <p><input type="submit" value="GO">
        <input type="reset"
value="CLEAR"></p>
      </form>
    <hr size=2 width=100% NOSHADE>
  </BODY>
  </HTML>
```

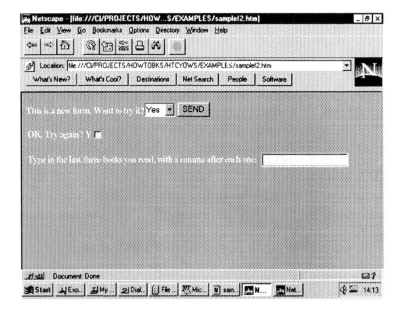

Fig. 17. Sample form 2.

Sample form 2 (Figure 17)

```
<HTML>
<HEAD><TITLE>Sample form 2</TITLE></HEAD>
<BODY bgcolor="gray" text="#ffffff">
   </FORM>
   <FORM ACTION="#next">
   <P>
   This is a new form. Want to try it?<SELECT
   NAME="Menu1">
   <OPTION>Yes
   <OPTION>No</SELECT>  <INPUT  TYPE="SUBMIT"
   VALUE="SEND">
   <P>
   <A NAME="next"></A>OK. Try again? Y<INPUT
   TYPE="CHECKBOX" NAME="Check1">
   <P>
   Type in the last three books you read, with a
   comma after each one:
   <INPUT NAME="Books3" VALUE=""MAXLENGTH="60">
   </FORM>
  </BODY>
</HTML>
```

Sample form 3 (Figure 18)

```
<HTML>
<HEAD><TITLE>Sample form 3</TITLE></HEAD>
<BODY TEXT="red">
<CENTER><H1>Form Example 3</H1></CENTER>
<CENTER><h2>This is two forms in the same HTML
document.</H2></CENTER><P>
<HR size=6 width=33% shade="blue">
   <FORM METHOD="POST" ACTION="http://hoohoo.
   ncsa.uiuc.edu/cgi-bin/post-query">
   Here is the first form:<P>
   Text entry (INPUT) field #1: <INPUT NAME="INPUT1">
   Text  entry  field  #2:  <INPUT  SIZE=10
```

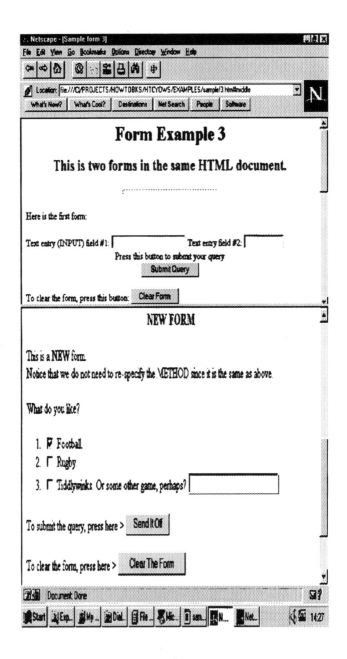

Fig. 18. Sample form 3.

```
NAME="INPUT2">
  <center>Press this button to submit your
  query: <br><INPUT TYPE="submit"
  VALUE="Submit Query"> </center><P>
  To clear the form, press this button: <INPUT
  TYPE="reset" VALUE="Clear Form">.
  </FORM>
<FONT COLOR="#006000"><A NAME="middle"></
a><HR>
<H3><CENTER>NEW FORM</CENTER></H3>
  <FORM ACTION="http://hoohoo.ncsa.uiuc.edu/
  cgi-bin/query">
  This is a <B>NEW </B> form.<br> Notice that we
  do not need to re-specify the METHOD since it
  is the same as above.<P>
  What do you like? <OL>
  <LI><INPUT TYPE="checkbox" NAME="check1"
  VALUE="Football" checked>Football.
  <LI><INPUT TYPE="checkbox" NAME="check2"
  VALUE="Rugby"> Rugby.
  <LI><INPUT TYPE="checkbox" NAME="check3">
  Tiddlywinks. Or some other game,perhaps?
  <INPUT NAME="other_game" SIZE=25>
  </OL><P>
  To submit the query, press here > <INPUT
  TYPE="submit" VALUE="Send It Off">. <P>
  To clear the form, press here &gt <INPUT
  TYPE="reset" VALUE="Clear The Form">.
  </FONT></FORM><HR><P>
<A HREF="#TOP">Back to the top</A> or <A
HREF="#middle">back to the top of this one</
A>.<P>
</BODY>
</HTML>
```

Notice these things about Sample form 3.

- You were able to change the text colour by specifying it once as Red with <BODY TEXT="firstcolour">...</BODY> which surrounds the entire document and respecifying it with <FONT COLOR="secondcolour">...</Font> for the second form.

- You inserted an anchor tag for 'middle' which takes you to the beginning of the new form by clicking the hypertext at the end. There was no need to specify 'top'.

- The INPUT field for Football is CHECKED by default. Football and Rugby have VALUEs included. See what difference this makes when you get the response back.

- There are two lines which use a > sign as text. The first is:

To submit the query, press here >

This character was entered with the > key. However, it is possibly best to avoid characters HTML uses for particular purposes. In the second line:

To clear the form, press here >

This was entered as &gt using the special character escape sequence.

Sample form 4 (Figure 19)

```
<HTML
<HEAD><TITLE>Sample form 4</TITLE></HEAD>
<BODY><H1><CENTER>HIDDEN TEXT</center></H1>
   <FORM METHOD="POST" ACTION="mailto:(your own
   e-mail address)">
      <Table BORDER><TR ALIGN=CENTER BGCOLOR=
      "#8888EE">
      <TD COLSPAN=40 BGCOLOR="yellow"><B>HIDDEN
      </B></TD>
      <TD><INPUT NAME="anything"></TD>
      <TD>Text input field - type anything </TD>
      <TD COLSPAN=40 BGCOLOR="yellow"><B>=TEXT
      </B></TD></TR>
      <INPUT TYPE="hidden" NAME="hidden1" VALUE=
      "v1"></P>
   </table><P>
```

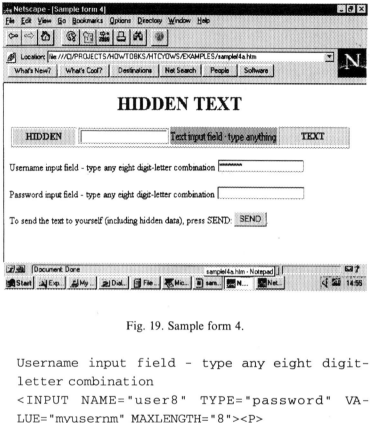

Fig. 19. Sample form 4.

```
Username input field - type any eight digit-
letter combination
<INPUT NAME="user8" TYPE="password" VA-
LUE="myusernm" MAXLENGTH="8"><P>
<font align="right">Password input field - type
any eight digit-letter combination
<INPUT NAME="pass8" TYPE="password" MAX-
LENGTH="8"></font>
   <P>To send the text to yourself (including
   hidden data), press SEND :
   <INPUT TYPE="submit" VALUE="SEND"><P>
   </FORM >
</BODY> </HTML>
```

- Notice how the first input box and its text are set within a table. You can hide the border to make it look like a centred input box. However, TABLE also gives the possibility to use colour.

- Two sets of hidden elements are specified here with different NAME/VALUE attributes. You would use one or the other in different HTML documents if, for example, you wanted to gather data on two different days, or two different users were collecting information. Hidden elements are not displayed in the document but they are not secret (like a password). Use View Document Source to see them.

- The Username and Password fields are slightly different. In one there is a VALUE. If this is not overtyped, it will be sent as the username "myusernm". The Password field is empty, ready for input. Both are echoed by a series of asterisks (********) whatever is typed, and they remain secret. You may have seen this sort of combination in your dial-up connection, where the user name is already entered (but displays as asterisks) and the Password field is empty.

USING A FORM TO DETERMINE WHICH BROWSER

You can use a script written in Java (a programming language used in HTML) within a form to find out if a viewer is using Netscape (2.0 and above) or Internet Explorer (3.0 and above). It uses the navigator.userAgent object to determine the browser type, which can only be interrogated (using non CGI scripts) for these two browsers. This is useful if your page uses a lot of elements specific to one or other browser. You can include two versions of any HTML code within different Web page documents and re-route the viewer to the correct document, depending on their browser type. This prevents the frustration of a viewer not being able to see your Web page in its full glory because it was written with browser-specific tags.

Let's say you have two versions of a Web page – one specific for Internet Explorer (msiever1.htm). These will be loaded from the first document presented (say, homepage.htm). Putting the following script in homepage.htm will determine whether the user is using Internet Explorer or not.

```
< FORM >
<P>
<INPUT TYPE="button" NAME="Browser Check"
VALUE="Check the Browser"
```

```
onClick="check()">
</FORM>
  <SCRIPT LANGUAGE="JavaScript">
  function check()
  {
  var BrowserType=navigator.userAgent;
  if (BrowserType.indexOf("MSIE") == 25)
     {location.href="msiever1.html"}
  else { location.href="check.html"}
  }
  </SCRIPT>
```

The button, when clicked, runs the function check() in the Java script. This checks the navigator.userAgent object presented to the server by the browser to see whether "MSIE" is at the 25th position in the navigator.userAgent string. If it is, then the browser loads the page msiever1.html (a Web page you have written with Internet Explorer in mind) or else it loads check.html. This works because Internet Explorer (3.0 beta 2, Windows 95) and Netscape (3.0 beta 5, Windows 95) will each present a string to check.html. These are, respectively:

```
Mozilla/2.0 (compatible;MSIE 3.OA;Windows 95)
Mozilla/3.Ob5 (Win95;1)
```

Notice that in the Internet Explorer string, if:

```
(BrowserType.indexOf("MSIE") == 25)
```

MSIE starts at the 25th character. That's what the Java script looks for. If it is there, the browser is MSIE (Microsoft Internet Explorer).

SUMMARY

- Forms can be used to collect information such as mailing addresses, credit card numbers and answers to questions.

- They also give a web page an interactive feel – the user actually does something.

9
Getting Framed

ADDING FLEXIBILITY WITH FRAMES

Frames add flexibility to Web pages. They are a way of dividing the Web page area into more or less independent sub-areas, each one with its own behaviour; for example:

- each frame has a separate URL loaded into it (you are viewing two or more different Web pages or images)
- all frames can be resized automatically when the visible area changes size and manual resizing by the user can be on or off
- a frame can have its own NAME, so it can be referenced by links
- a frame can stay in view independently of what is happening to the rest of the Web page
- a frame can scroll.

This means, for instance, that information or images you want to stay in view constantly (a title image, a banner, navigation buttons, contents, results of a search or whatever) can be held in a 'static' frame which never changes while the user is retrieving information to and moving through the 'live' frame.

FRAME replaces BODY
The basic command for frames is <FRAMESET>...</FRAME-SET> which acts very like the familiar <BODY>...</BODY> tags and **replaces** these. A basic document would look like this:

```
<HTML>
<HEAD><TITLE>....</TITLE>
</HEAD>
   <FRAMESET>
```

```
<FRAME SRC="homepage.htm">
  </FRAMESET>
</HTML>
```

This would set up a document with one frame, which contains the document "homepage.htm". Why would you want to do that when you could just have displayed the homepage document? You wouldn't necessarily, but you could have two, three or more things going on in a framed document that you couldn't in a standard Web page.

EXAMPLES OF FRAMES

Try this example. Type in these commands and save the document as frame1.htm.

```
<HTML>
<HEAD>
<TITLE><H1>Frame Document 1</H1></TITLE>
</HEAD>
  <FRAMESET ROWS="80,3*,*,60">
    <FRAME NORESIZE NAME="doctitle" SCROLLING=
    "no" SRC="doctitle.htm">
      <FRAMESET COLS="30%,70%">
      <FRAME NAME="contents" SCROLLING="yes"
      SRC="contents.htm">
      <FRAME NAME="homepage"  SCROLLING="yes"
      SRC="homepage.htm">
      </FRAMESET>
    <FRAME NAME="navigate" NORESIZE SCROLLING=
    "no" SRC="navigate.htm">
    <FRAME NAME="e-mail" NORESIZE SCROLLING=
    "no" SRC="e-mail.htm">
  <NOFRAMES>
```
(This would contain all the same information, as if there were no frames)
```
  </NOFRAMES>
```

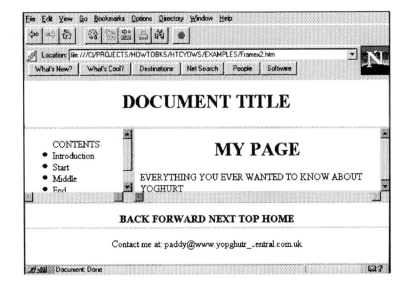

Fig. 20. A document with frames.

```
</FRAMESET>
</HTML>
```

These frames are 'nested' – one within another. This will look like the illustration in Figure 20 once text is added.

Notice that, in Netscape Editor, you do not see any of this information and a document containing frames cannot be manipulated in Editor – you have to access the source code in Notepad.

Putting web pages in your frames

You will need to construct five other documents corresponding to:

- doctitle.htm

- contents.htm

- homepage.htm

- navigate.htm

- e-mail.htm.

Put anything you like in them – the frames will be the same shape and size as those shown but the content will depend on you. They should have normal HTML elements between <BODY>...</BODY> tags.

COMMANDS WITHIN FRAMESET

Nothing apart from HEAD information should appear before the <FRAMESET> tag otherwise the frames will be ignored completely. The <FRAMESET> tag can have row or columns attributes:

```
<FRAMESET rows="height in pixels or percentages"
```

for example:

```
<FRAMESET rows="60,*,80">
```

This would set up three rows, the top and bottom ones 60 pixels high and the middle one of whatever size is left to occupy. Note that you did not have to specify three rows, as HTML worked this out from the fact that there were three values in the ROWS= attribute. Specifying pixel height can lead to complications when viewing since a user may not have the viewing area set up to the same size as you did when developing the page. It may be best to use relative values (percentages) as follows.

```
<FRAMESET rows="10%,2*,*,10%">
```

This would establish four rows, the second occupying 40 per cent (2/3 of 100-10-20-10) and the third 20 per cent (1/3) of the remaining visible area. Height values can be mixed, so that a syntax like <FRAMESET ROWS="100,*10%> is possible. You might want to specify an absolute row height for a graphic, for example.

```
<FRAMESET COLS="column width in pixels or
percentages">
```

Everything that applies to rows applies to columns.

Between the <FRAMESET>...</FRAMESET> tags you can only have <FRAME> tags, a <NOFRAMES> tag or other nested <FRAMESET>...</FRAMESET> tags. Just as tables can be nested inside tables (but not forms within forms), you can have frames within frames.

In the example above you set up four rows with <FRAMESET ROWS="80,3*,*,60"> the first row 80 pixels high and the last 60 pixels high, with the next two rows taking up 3/4 and 1/4 of the remaining space respectively.

The two column frames were specified with a nested `<FRAMESET>...</FRAMESET>`. Within row two, you set up two columns with `<FRAMESET COLS="30%,70%">...</FRAMESET>`. They contain scrolling frames called contents.htm and mypage.htm.

Frames within frames

`<FRAME>` defines a single frame, and there should be one of these tags per frame created with `<FRAMESET>`. There are six possible attributes (eight in Internet Explorer) you can use within a `<FRAME>` tag:

- `<FRAME NAME="whatever">` – this will give a reference name "whatever" to the frame.

- `<FRAME SRC="...">` – this specifies the source of a URL (a document or an image) to include in the frame.

- `<FRAME SCROLLING="yes/no/auto">` – this tells the frame whether or not to have a scroll bar. The values "yes" and "no" are obvious, and "auto" allows the browser to choose whether the chosen contents fit the frame size without a scrollbar or whether one will be needed. The default is "auto" so think about whether you always want or always don't want a scrollbar.

- `<FRAME NORESIZE>` – when you define a frame a viewer can resize it by dragging on the frame border, resizing other frames in the process. If you don't want your beautifully balanced Web page to pulled about, use the NORESIZE attribute (no value). If any frame next to an edge is non-resizable, that edge cannot be moved so other, touching frames cannot be resized. All frames are resizable by default.

- `<FRAME MARGINHEIGHT="pixels">` – this attribute fixes the top and bottom margins of a frame. MARGINHEIGHT is optional. All frames by default let the browser decide the margin spacing, as in the example above but MARGINHEIGHT="0" is not allowed.

- `<FRAME MARGINWIDTH="pixels">` – the MARGINWIDTH attribute is exactly like MARGINHEIGHT for spacing to the sides of the frame.

For Internet Explorer

Internet Explorer adds two more attributes:

- `<FRAME FRAMEBORDER="yes/no">` – Microsoft Internet Explorer allows control of the frame border. If "no", the borders for that frame are not shown.

- `<FRAME FRAMESPACING="pixels">` – Internet Explorer permits space (like an invisible border) around a frame and the "pixels" value is the distance around the frame in pixels. This creates the appearance of a 'floating' frame with text around it.

Non-frame-capable browsers

At the time of writing, frames are only supported by Netscape 2.0 and above and Internet Explorer 3.0 and above. Some aspects of frames are only available in Internet Explorer. It is a good general rule not to design Web pages so that certain browsers can't read them, and not every browser is frame-capable. The `<NOFRAMES>` . . .`</NOFRAMES>` tags envelope additional or alternative content viewable by these browsers. A frame-capable browser will ignore everything between these tags, which will contain a non-frame version of the same text as your frames. If that sounds like writing the Web page twice, you're right. But what could be more frustrating that finding a page you can't read and a sniffy message telling you that you ought to grow up and get a better browser? Be thoughtful!

MAKING FURTHER REFINEMENTS

- Try editing the frame document above and its constituent parts. Make the contents list in contents.htm into clickable links to other documents called intro.htm, start.htm, etc.

- Change the navigate.htm document so it contains clickable buttons.

- Instead of DOCUMENT TITLE in doctitle.htm, insert an image as follows:

  `<IMG SRC="newimage.gif">`

  and create an image 640 wide x 80 high. Try it at a different size and see what happens.

- Make your e-mail.htm document contain a clickable link to your e-mail address or another URL.

SUMMARY

- Frames allow you to hold one part of a display static while others move. This is useful for keeping certain information (a site index or navigation links) in view at all times.

- Each frame contains a separate HTML document.

- Some browsers still do not support frames, so you may need to think about also presenting your information in a non-frames version.

- Frames can be made with or without scrolling, resizing and borders, allowing you to determine the look of your page.

FINDING HELP WITH FRAMES

If you find the whole issue of frames HTML tags too confusing, there is a useful program called Framegang from Sausage software which can help with this at *http://www.sausage.com/store/download/ dl_snagletpack.html)*. Make sure you get the Windows 95 or Windows 3.x version.

10
Designing Your Web Page

KNOWING WHAT YOU KNOW

You now know how to:

- write HTML documents
- use font and text effects
- add in-line and external images
- put links into your document
- use tables
- get information with forms
- use frames.

Now you could construct a Web page or a series of pages. But these will have to be designed.

ENCOURAGING GOOD WRITING AND DESIGN

You will have heard somewhere, usually on the radio when some Member of Parliament for the eighteenth century is braying on about educational standards, that computers are ruining our children's ability to read, write and count. This is rubbish. Cinema is considered a valid art form but you don't even need to be able to read when you go to the pictures. Computers encourage literacy, numeracy and self-expression. To use, and especially to create for, computers you need to be able to do the following:

- spell and use grammar and syntax
- count above 10 without taking your socks off
- think logically.

Computer scientists and scientists in general, contrary to the popular imagination, are logical, well-read, can spell correctly (most of the time) and use proper sentences. Spelling, syntax and order are the lifeblood of computing since any program code that is full of errors just doesn't run and if it's constructed sloppily it may run but it will take forever. Readability means spelling, grammar, punctuation and logical order, but it also means how information is presented and whether your background colour makes your page easy or hard to read.

JUDGING WHAT IS GOOD AND BAD

It's impossible to say what makes a good or bad Web page design, since these judgments are aesthetic, subjective and individual. But there are some general guidelines. As someone who comes across your page on the web, I should:

- be immediately attracted to it
- want to return to it again
- want to tell others about it
- be sufficiently impressed to want to copy it and examine your source code ('How did she do THAT?').

Create or capture

There are naturally talented designers out there. You may or may not be one of them. However, you will look at a lot of Web pages. If you see something you like, swipe the idea. Either save the web page to your hard disk and disembowel it later to see what makes it tick, or take a screen capture (press Print Screen) and save it in a graphics program so that you can look at it in more detail. This is not to say you can steal other Web designers' images, but you can copy their ideas, see how the HTML code operates and replicate those aspects you think will work for you.

There are many pages on the web at college and university sites which offer tips on design. But what it comes down to is: What do you like? What don't you like?

POINTS TO BEAR IN MIND WHEN CONSTRUCTING YOUR WEB PAGE

Think about backgrounds

Make your page visually appealing – too many clashing colours or a messy layout may put viewers off. Different audiences have different perspectives, though. For a good, free tutorial on design for different audiences, go down to your local newsagent and compare various magazine covers. A top-notch ladies mag like *Cosmopolitan* or *Harpers & Queens* is saying something very different from a heavy metal music publication or a children's comic.

Style magazines are cool, sophisticated, pastel-coloured with large, aspirational images and clean type. Rock mags look as if someone's tipped an art-room dustbin on to a piece of paper. And that's on purpose. Remember that magazine covers appeal not to people but to what people want to be. That's why you have to design your Web page for what the audience thinks of itself. The Art Editor of *The Beano* is probably a talented, sensitive soul who paints watercolours at the weekend, but he/she knows his/her job and has designed the comic perfectly to suit the audience of wannabe Dennis The Menaces.

Using simple colours

Keep your design and colours simple. Not everybody uses the same Web browser as you do and some are still trying to get along with a steam-driven browser cobbled up in a computer science class in 1993. Different Web browsers (and even different versions of the same browser) can only read older versions of HTML. So your mega-technicolour background will look super at home but execrable to someone with another browser, different graphics capability and so on.

Some browsers don't recognise certain HTML tags, such as CENTER or FRAMESET, which can disturb your neat layout. You can't legislate for all this, but bear it in mind or at the very least include some sort of 'I know' notice in your Web page like: 'This document is best viewed with Netscape 2.0 or better.'

Having loads of images in thousands of colours will also slow down the loading of your page and the viewer may get bored long before your fantastic design gets a chance to unfold itself.

Remember that somebody has to read your Web page. Out there in cyberspace there are the most unreadable pages which may contain information that would make everyone's life easier or more wonderful, but no one ever stays long enough to find out. Ask someone to look at your page and comment critically. You may lose a friend, but you'll gain wisdom and that is a gift beyond any price.

If you have access to a school or college, talk to teachers in the Art and English departments. They will give you valuable advice (which will often be contradictory, but that's life).

Don't be a space cadet

Use equal spacing between text lines of equal importance and more spacing before new categories of text. In other words, use spacing as a visual guide to the viewer as to what goes together and what is separate, new or different.

Get some style

Write yourself a style guide – decide on spacing between heading and text, between subheadings and text and major text elements or section, and stick to it. If you are using Internet Assistant or a Web authoring tool you can build these into your template by altering the default styles. You could set up all your new styles in a template web page called mynormal.htm and start from there when you want to design a new page.

Web authoring programs will have style guides or similar Setup options. If you are writing HTML directly with Notepad or another text editor, just write down your style guide and stick to it.

This is not to say your styles will be reproduced faithfully in every browser, however, so don't rely on it.

Form follows function

The way your Web page looks should reflect what it's for. Some of the best and most-visited Web pages are no more than lists of hyperlinks on a dark background. Others, especially instruction manuals, help files and so on, are properly laid out documents that would look just as good when printed. Others again have forms, tables and frames, but for a purpose.

Use consistent emphasis

Bullets, bold, underlining and italic are fine and useful, but don't overdo the text effects. Remember what happened at primary school when you underlined everything and wrote the really, really important bits in capitals or with green ink. You probably got a telling off for it then, and you'd deserve one if you did it in a Web page. Don't use emphasisers at all unless you really have to and set yourself some rules as to when you use them and for what. These might include the following:

• Bullets introduce major new sections of text.

• Bold is only in titles and section headings.

• Underlining is only for instructional text ('Read this') and for hyperlinks ('My e-mail address').

- Italic is only for references to URLs ('*See http.//www.bozo.co.uk/ mystyles.htm*').

- Use heading levels to organise your Web page – H1 for the title, H2 for the section headings, etc.

Spelling and grammar matter

Do not go out with a misspelt or ungrammatical Web page. Check it thoroughly – and that does not mean running it past a spellchecker which won't, for instance, tell you the difference between its and it's; there, their and they're; who's and whose; your and you're and apostrophised plurals. Just so there's no misunderstanding, here are the rules:

- 'It's' means 'it is' and 'its' means 'belonging to it'. You write 'John's' and 'the web's' but 'his' and 'its'.

- 'There' is the opposite of 'here', 'their' means 'belonging to them' and 'they're' means 'they are'.

- 'Who's' is short for 'who is' as in 'who's at the door' but 'whose' means 'belonging to whom' – 'A man whose day has come'.

- 'You're' means 'you are' and 'your' means 'belonging to you' as in 'you're on your way'.

In case you're unfamiliar with the apostrophised plural, it's also known as 'the Grocer's S'. Look at the signs in almost any shop window and you'll see endless examples of POTATO'S or VIDEO'S or MOT'S. These are plurals and should not have apostrophes except in sentences like 'The potato's attacked my cat', 'The video's on fire' or 'Your MOT's run out'.

Check for grammar, too. The world is going to be reading your page and why should they get the impression you're a witless moron? Likewise, hold back on the punctuation. Try and avoid completely exclamation marks, question marks, semicolons, colons (except in http: of course), ellipsis (using dots to indicate an unfinished sentence, like 'wait for the beep...') and heavy use of brackets (which no one likes (and can (sometimes) look (sort of) ugly)).

If you genuinely have trouble with spelling and grammar, ask someone to check your Web page – print it off if necessary.

Using the right tags

Make sure you know what markup tag is producing what result. Use the link element `<A HREF="...">Text</A>` to make links but the `<U>Text</U>` tag for underlining and the `< I >Text </I>` tag for italicising. Do not use `<TITLE>Text</TITLE>` just to put something in a large, bold font – use `<B>Text</B>` instead.

Using fewer lines

Horizontal lines (which you enter with the markup tab `< HR >`) are greatly overused and should be restricted to page breaks (full width lines) and section breaks (half width lines).

Providing alternatives to graphics

Not everyone's browser is graphical. Lynx is a good example of a popular non-graphical browser. Where you use graphics include the ALT text as well as saying what the graphic is – 'Picture of me' or 'Next button'.

Helping viewers to navigate

Not all browsers can do back and forward navigation easily. Netscape can and it caches viewed documents (stores them temporarily in a \netscape\cache subdirectory so that they can be retrieved without another download) but other browsers may not do this. Put links like Next, Back, Home, Top, Bottom at the foot of each page, both as clickable graphics and as clickable text.

Sometimes just including a text line like 'Use the Back button to return here' is a help.

There are Web sites you can get totally lost in and never find the start again. Every page should, ideally, have relative links to every other page on your site plus Back and Forward links. These are not the same as the Back and Forward arrows on the browser toolbar (which take you up and down the history list) but hyperlinks that help the user navigate through your documents in sequential order.

By using a combination of your Back (a hyperlink to the previous page in the sequence) and the browser's Back (which goes to the last page looked at) everyone will be able to get around fine. And if you have a complete set of links in every page, so much the better.

What to include in personal Web pages

It is often said that personal Web pages should include:

- a picture of the author

- the name of the author

- for whom he or she works

- hobbies

- personal description

- contact addresses, phone numbers and e-mail

and for academics and students

- research interests

- list of publications.

The picture, hobbies and personal details can get a bit sickly, but then, we're British. We don't want to know what you look like or whether you do macramé. If it's macramé you're after, list yourself on some on-line directory's Macramé sub-class. There must be one.

If, however, you want a good laugh, go and look for the personal Web pages of American families – they always have a nice photo of Mom, Dad and the kids plus dog and sometimes, just sometimes, they're all in a Jacuzzi. Web flashing, it is called, and it's sad.

Warning! Offensive material! Site under construction!
Sadly, there is a lot of offensive text and graphics out there on the web – don't add to it as it gives us all a bad name. Nobody wants mucky words or pictures sprung on them when demonstrating their new web site to their Auntie. Equally, don't give any viewers nasty surprises.

- Make sure viewers know what they're in for in terms of content.

- If a new page is taking a while to sort out, then say so.

- If you're trying out a form or a bit of 3-D and it's not finished yet, issue a warning.

- If a link leads to a three-hour 25 Mb download make sure that's obvious.

- Just saying 'Page Under Development' is not enough. Explain when it will be ready.

- And if you do happen to have any pictures of you and the happy family in the Jacuzzi, tell potential viewers that's the case so there are no shocks.

Graphics, audio, video, forms, etc.

Your wonderful Web page has forms to fill in, clickable graphics, bits of video, Shockwaved animation, four frames per page and the like. Is it all necessary? Or are you just showing off? They all take time to download. Solve this one by having links to such things which people can choose to go to or not go to.

Making it browsable

You don't need to put all your information on one page, but you can. You can use hyperlinks to get viewers around to bite-sized chunks in separate HTML documents that fit into a browser window (about half a page of A4). Or you can have one big page with lots of relative links to places on that page.

The difference is that one big page takes longer to load at first but is a doddle to skip around in, whereas having lots of little pages means lots of short waits for loading. It's up to you.

Giving them something to do

Most people like jumping around in a site and having lots of mouse clicking to do. It's more fun than just reading and it makes them feel in control. Others don't like it. But what's sure is that nobody wants to be confronted with a slab of unorganised text. Put in lots of keyword links to other part of the same document, or to other documents in your Web site.

Keeping it consistent

You will see a lot of Web sites consisting of pages that just don't look as if they belong together. This is very off-putting. Try to use the same background and text styles on each page, use the same layouts for paragraphs and keep images roughly the same size, look and background colour.

Including useful links

You will no doubt want to direct people to another Web site. Put in links that consist of some meaningful name ('For more info on steel washers click here') and also the appropriate URL ('at *http.// www.anorak.com/washers.html#favourites*'). Some people like to write down URLs. Yes, with a pencil. One of the best things about other people's Web pages is that they will have found links you never would have. So if you see something in your area of interest you think might be useful to others, put in a link to it, say what it is and list the URL.

Linking your Web pages

If you find other Web sites that include interests or businesses like yours, ask if you can have your Web page linked in these. See Chapter 12 for more information.

Keeping your links live

Check your links. Sometimes they go dead or are moved to another server. If a link is not active it will generate Error 404 (file not found) which is immensely frustrating for viewers. If you don't have a file or script to link to but there will be a link at some point, change the link to some emphasised text. Most graphical Web browsers use underlining and colour for hyperlinks but textual browsers use reversed-out text for both links and underlines. Change the link declaration

```
<A HREF="...">Text</A> to <U>Text</U>
```

the underline marking and tell viewers the link isn't ready yet. When your link is ready, hyperlink it and change the text.

Signing your pages

Somebody, somewhere, some time is going to save or print your Web page. What if you don't have your name and e-mail address on that particular page? Put them on every page or at the very least on the welcome (first) page.

Keeping it up

There is nothing worse than a dead site. Update it regularly with something new or interesting and say so ('Last updated ...'). As a rule of thumb, visit your own site weekly, check all the links and upload the first page again with a new 'updated' date. Put in new information regularly and say so.

Testing your page

You'd be amazed how many Web authors create a site on their computer at home and never upload it and check it out with their browser to see if they can get to it and if it makes any sense at all. Do this, please. Better still, try it from a variety of machines with different browsers – get down to the local college or library, who may let you have half an hour's free access time. Or go to a CyberCafé, have a nice cuppa and access your Web page from there.

DECIDING THE BEST TIME TO DESIGN YOUR WEB PAGE

The best time is **now**. You'll never do it otherwise. But if you're really looking for a good time to engage in this fascinating, frustrating and fulfilling pastime, try Sunday afternoon. There is a time on a Sunday when you've had two breakfasts, read all the papers, taken as many baths as the human frame can withstand, walked the dog, drunk more tea than is healthy and cut your toenails. There's nothing on the TV except Harry Secombe or men's hockey and nowhere is open.

That is a good time to start constructing your very own Web page. Go to it!

MOVING ON

If you put this book down now, you would be able to design a creditable Web page. The rest contains information on more advanced aspects that you may want to tackle once you have mastered the basics.

11
Livening Up Your Web Pages
with Video and Sound

ADDING VIDEO

HTML documents can have video embedded within them. The procedures are rather different for Netscape, Internet Explorer and Mosaic.

Netscape

Netscape makes use of the <EMBED> tag to put objects, including video, into an HTML page. Internet Explorer can use this too, so there may be no need to use the <IMG SRC=" . . . " DYNSRC= " . . . " . . . > line at all. The syntax for embedding is:

```
<EMBED SRC= "object.ext">
```

where object.ext is the filename of the embedded object.

In fact, <EMBED> extremely flexible and allows you to add objects of any type, including documents and sound (see below). The viewer must have an application which can use the data (such as Word for a document or mplayer.exe for an AVI movie file) or have a Netscape or Internet Explorer plug-in that can manipulate the embedded file format.

The <EMBED> tag is more or less the same as <IMG>, and uses the WIDTH, HEIGHT, BORDER, HSPACE and VSPACE attributes. A typical line might be:

```
<EMBED  SRC="play.avi"  WIDTH=64  HEIGHT=64
ALIGN=RIGHT BORDER=0>
```

Netscape plug-ins

Netscapes plug-ins use the <EMBED> element. Plug-ins are programs associated with a particular file type that Netscape cannot handle directly, like an extension to a power tool. If Netscape comes across a file of unknown type it will search for a plug-in associated with that file type and use it to display or modify the object.

New versions of Netscape come with some plug-ins already installed, including plug-ins for audio, video, VRML 'worlds' and QT (quicktime) movies. Information about plug-ins, and access to more plug-ins, are available from the Netscape site at *http://home.netscape.com/*. Some plug-ins have extra attributes which will be in the documentation files downloaded with the plug-in.

Use Netscape plug-ins for Internet Explorer
Internet Explorer Version 3.0 supports Netscape plug-ins by using either the correct plug-in, or a control called ActiveX to display the object. ActiveX modules are like plug-ins, but specific to Internet Explorer. ActiveVRML and ActiveMovie add-ons for Internet Explorer can display VRML worlds, AVI, QT, MPEG video, WAV audio, Sun AU and AIFF sound files, using the correct ActiveX <OBJECT> tag, or the <EMBED> tag used by Netscape plug-ins.

Internet Explorer
Microsoft's browser allows .AVI video clips to be embedded. This is done within the <IMG> tag but there are particular attributes to add in place of the SRC= attribute to make this happen. DYNSRC (Dynamic Source) does this job, but SRC= can be used to give non-video-enabled browsers a still image to display instead. A typical line would be:

```
<IMG SRC="still.gif" DYNSRC="play.avi" WIDTH=64
HEIGHT=64 START=MOUSEOVER CONTROLS LOOP=3 LOOP-
DELAY=1000 ALIGN=RIGHT>
```

Making a still from a video
SRC="still.gif" specifies a static GIF image that can be played in a non-video-playing browser.

DYNSRC="play.avi" embeds the video file called play.avi within a pane. It would be neat if still.gif were the first frame of play.avi and there's no reason why that can't be so.

Open Windows Media Player (windows\mplayer.exe), open a .AVI file and without starting it, click Edit Copy Object. Now open a graphics package and Edit Paste. This will paste in the first frame as a still image. Now you can save it as a GIF or JPG file with an appropriate name (such as still.gif).

Play immediately or wait
START=MOUSEOVER tells the clip to play when the mouse cursor passes over the image. An alternative is START=FILEOPEN (the default if you leave out START=), which starts the clip playing as soon as the file is opened (immediately). You can specify both so that the clip starts again when the cursor crosses it.

Controls and loops
If you include CONTROLS within the tag, a control panel is displayed under the pane which lets the viewer pause, skip or restart the video if desired.

LOOP determines how many times a clip will play. Setting LOOP=-1, or LOOP=INFINITE plays the video in an indefinite loop.

LOOPDELAY tells the browser how long to wait between loops, in milliseconds. LOOPDELAY=1000 specifies a one-second gap between loops.

ALIGN, HEIGHT and WIDTH apply to the video, just as they do to the <IMG> tag.

Using <OBJECT> in Internet Explorer
Internet Explorer supports a new tag – <OBJECT> — as a way of controlling ActiveX (see below) and other objects in HTML documents. It takes over from the <IMG> tag but extends these to more than just still graphic images. However, Netscape plug-ins can be used by Internet Explorer and it is simpler to stick with <EMBED> for all purposes.

Video files are large
In-line video (where the video plays in the Web page rather than downloads to the viewer's PC) can take a long time to load and play and can be extremely jerky. It works best on fast PCs connected to a high bandwidth server and for animations with a few colours rather than a real movie.

If you want to make movies available, show a thumbnail of a still taken from the video and link it to a downloadable movie file. (See Making a still from a video, above.) The simplest method of achieving this is to have the movie as the sole item within the body of a separate HTML document and display a related gif. This requires a line such as:

```
<img src="http://www.goodpics.com.uk/gifs/
imagela.gif" width=60 height=60><BR><A
```

```
HREF="videola.htm">Click here to download vi-
deo</a>
```

The still is imagela.gif and the text below it is hyperlinked to the
document videola.htm which contains only the video object.

SOUNDING OFF WITH SOUND ON

The <EMBED> tag can also be used to play background (in-line)
sound or to play specific sounds when, for example, a button is
pressed. The <EMBED> tag tells Netscape to play a sound. The
equivalent tag for Internet Explorer is <BGSOUND> and for Mosaic
is <SOUND>. Put all of these in a document to tell all three browsers
(and others) to play the sound.

Background sound
You may well have a MIDI file called canyon.mid in your
\windows\media directory. If not, search for other files with the
extensions .mid. Double-clicking on any one in File Manager or
Windows Explorer will open mplayer.exe and play the sound file. If
you embed any of these sound files in a Web page, the viewer's
browser will play them (if it is set up correctly). Try this in a
document and make sure the sound files are in the same directory:

```
<EMBED SRC="canyon.mid" HIDDEN="True">
<BGSOUND SRC="canyon.mid">
<SOUND SRC="canyon.wav">
```

This will play the sound file canyon.mid in Netscape and Internet
Explorer and a similar .wav file in Mosaic. The three browsers have
some other differences.

Netscape
See earlier in this chapter for more <EMBED> attributes which
control width, height, etc. The HIDDEN="True" attribute in the
<EMBED> element tells Netscape not to display the controls for the
sound file. Leave it out or change it to HIDDEN-"false" to see
the controls. You can also add LOOP=n attribute which will
determine how many times a sound plays. If $n=-1$ or
LOOP=INFINITE the sound will play indefinitely. DELAY=n will
delay the sound by n seconds.

Internet Explorer

Internet Explorer sees the <BGSOUND> tag and plays the sound file in the background. Sounds played by Internet Explorer with <BGSOUND> can be .wav, .au or .mid formats. Use LOOP=n and DELAY=s as with Netscape (above).

Mosaic

The < SOUND> element is only supported by Mosaic and plays .wav files. However, you can get Mosaic to use the <BGSOUND> tag for .mid files, but not in-line – it will launch an external application such as mplayer.exe. It will, however, play .wav files in-line using the <BGSOUND> tag. This could all get horribly complicated so decide what format your sound file will be, and use only the appropriate tags that will suit most browsers.

Play over the background

Other sound files can be put in your Web page document using <EMBED> and these will play over the background sound when started.

Activate your sound

You might prefer to have the sound start when you press a link. This line will do it:

```
<A href="canyon.mid">play</a>
```

It will open the control console for sounds in a new Netscape window. The viewer can the control the sounds.

Sounds on mouse passes

This is extremely childish, but good fun. How about having invisible areas within your Web page that cause a noise when the mouse passes over them? As usual, different browsers have different methods

Netscape
Netscape's LiveConnect technology and the LiveAudio plug-in (standard with Netscape 3.0) allow the following. It relies on Java Script again.

```
<EMBED  SRC="parp.wav"  NAME="parp"  WIDTH="1"
HEIGHT="2" MASTERSOUND>
  <A href="#gotcha" OnMouseOver="Play_()">link</A>
```

```
<SCRIPT LANGUAGE="JavaScript">
<!- -
function Play_(){
   document.parp.play(false);
   }
// - ->
</SCRIPT>
<BR>
<A NAME="GOTCHA">GOTCHA</A>
```

NAME and MASTERSOUND are specific attributes of the LiveAudio plug-in using LiveConnect functions. NAME="parp" gives a unique identifier to the plug-in. MASTERSOUND tells the browser to control the sound using a script (see below). WIDTH and HEIGHT are used to make the control console there, but almost invisible – do not change these settings. Why not use HIDDEN? Hide the console and the file will only be played once.

OnMouseOver calls the script Play_() when the mouse passes over the word "link". You could use OnCLick so the sound file plays when the link is clicked. At present, clicking will take the browser to the anchor "GOTCHA" which could be elsewhere in the document. The HREF= could be another document to load, or any other allowable object.

JavaScript plays the object in the current document name "parp" (the parp.wav file) via its plug-in and uses the Play function. It's up to you what parp.wav actually contains. Try any .wav file you have to start with. As an added nicety, the link could be almost invisible – make it a full stop, for instance:

```
<A href="#gotcha" OnMouseOver="Play_()">.</A>
```

Internet Explorer
The effect is not so good if the file is viewed with Internet Explorer because a control panel will be displayed, as always happens when Internet Explorer meets the <EMBED> tag. There is a way with Visual Basic and Internet Explorer, but it is immensely more complex and relies on the <OBJECT> tag.

Why bother?
Yes, it's trivial, but it has been used to good effect in a Web page

with a series of pictures of every instrument in an orchestra. When the mouse passes over an instrument, that instrument plays an appropriate note. The pictures are graphics each hyperlinked to a different .wav file. There is a particular six-year-old who loves it.

Do bear in mind, though, that loading a sound file takes time and can slow down the page. Loaded once, however, it will remain in the user's cache and play faster next time round.

12
Linking Your Web Page

FREE (OR AT LEAST CHEAP) ADVERTISING

Imagine you had a billboard advert in your home town, but wanted everyone in Birmingham to see it. You could have it reprinted and rent another billboard space in Birmingham, paying for both privileges. But suppose someone came to you and said 'I will put a button on every billboard in Birmingham that advertises products like yours so that anyone interested can press it and see your billboard back in Dunstable. And I won't charge you much.' You'd probably jump at it.

Linking sites on the Web provides much the same facility. You will have noticed that the Web pages you browse have links in them – words (usually highlighted in another colour or italicised) or graphics which take you to another Web page or even to another Web site entirely. When your cursor moves over the link, the shape changes, often to a hand. Somewhere in your browser window (in Netscape it's at the bottom of the window) the URL of the linked file or Web site is shown.

Why you should have links
The link has three advantages:

1. Each Web page can be quite short, reducing loading times.

2. You can jump around quickly on the Web with a mouse click on a highlighted word or phrase or a graphic without having to know beforehand or search for the page or site that interests you.

3. There is no need to recreate information on your Web site if it exists elsewhere and you can link to it.

Link to other Web sites
Of course, this also means that you can put links to your Web site into other people's pages, if they'll let you. So you can now get your

Web pages seen in places no one would necessarily have thought of looking for them. This can often be achieved free or at low cost and you don't have to make a new version of your page.

Likewise, if your Web page is an advert, you can place a link to it in some advertising sites. Say you have an advert on the pages of one service provider, but would like to have it more widely seen. You could contact a site which accepts links (they don't all, of course, and some are expensive) and pay the rate to have your Web page address listed in the appropriate directory section.

The reason some Web and FTP sites don't allow links is because they couldn't monitor or control what anyone, you and me included, puts on those sites. The high cost of some sites which do encourage links is precisely because they do want to monitor and vet your Web site, and this takes time, resources and people. However, there are some – Super Mall is an example – which don't mind. Break a law or a rule of etiquette, though, and you could find yourself disliked or even prosecuted.

To establish a link you can sometimes just type it into an electronic form on the Web page you are interested in linking to. In other cases, you will have to phone or fax your URL to the Web site SysOp (Systems Operator). The Web page concerned will tell you how. Typically you will be charged a monthly, quarterly or annual fee, sometimes with a special offer (a free month, say) but you save the set-up costs because your Web page is already set up elsewhere.

Free linkings
Often, local service providers have a free Web page – check if your tourist board, chamber of commerce, special interest group, local college, council or whatever offers this service. If it's free, it's worth doing.

LINKING TO MAJOR WEB SEARCHERS

Understanding search engines, spiders, crawlers and bots
Search engines search the Web using keywords you have entered. Lycos, Magellan, InfoSeek and AltaVista are examples. They work by using indexing software called robots, crawlers or spiders. These constantly 'crawl' the Web to search for new or updated Web pages and will follow links from URL to URL until they have visited every Web site on the Internet. They burrow into Web sites, index them and compile a database which is what users actually search. The search results pull up a URL, some kind of abstract and often

information on how highly rated the search result was (a figure like 91 per cent may appear next to the listing).

The crawler will record the full text of every page in the Web site plus all external links, so it could find your site whether you have registered your Web page URL or not. However, submitting your URL will help. This tells the crawler to visit and index your site instead of waiting for it to eventually locate you through one of your external links. The crawler will visit your site every so often to renew its information and take out dead or expired links.

Understanding how search engines differ from directories, announcement sites and guides

Directories
A real search engine only needs to know your Web address. If you are asked for a lot more information (abstracts, etc.) what you have is a directory, not a crawler.

A directory will only list your Web page URL if you register with it. They do not use indexing crawlers and may not know you are out there. There's nothing wrong with this, it just takes longer to fill out the registration form. Directories are subdivided into categories and you will probably have to choose the heading under which to submit your Web page.

Announcement sites
Next time you load your browser, you may see a change to some of the graphics, announcing 'What's New'. This is an announcement. Goodness knows how many new sites join the Web and USENET every day. The profusion of these has led to the construction of announcement sites that look for and list new Web pages, articles and resources joining the internet. A good place to start is *comp.infosystems.www.announce* if your site is non-commercial.

The announcements are carried for a certain time (days, often) but they are archived so anyone can access them. It is worth thinking about having your site announced if it is going to make a big splash. You can also look as often as you like at announcements and see who else is putting up pages like yours, or in subjects which interest you.

Computer magazines often have a 'What's New on the Web' feature which will take at least some of its information from announcements.

Guides and cool sites

Another feature of your Web browser is that it will have a 'What's Cool' or 'What's Hot' button, sometimes both. These are example of guides. They differ from announcements in that they review and sometimes rate sites, but only do so for a fraction of those submitted.

If you want your site listed as 'Cool' or 'Hot' (there should be a difference, but goodness knows what it might be), make sure it is 'rate-worthy'. If it is, and it gets rated, you may be offered the use of a special icon, a bit like a quality mark.

You will see these icons on Web pages you browse, or somewhere it may say 'Cool Site of the Day 12/2/1993' or something similar. It's a bit like a Blue Peter Badge. Most cool sites usually select one new Web site every day and Web site writers like this because a cool site attracts a lot of attention ('high traffic', as they say), for a short time. However, as an attention grabber, it can't be beat. Some people never look at them on principle because they just know they're going to be sold something. That's possibly a little harsh.

If someone hasn't actually given you one of these icons, **do not** swipe it from elsewhere and use it. That is very bad Netiquette.

GETTING YOUR WEB PAGE INDEXED

One way to make sure your Web site is seen is to have it known by a big, powerful searcher like AltaVista, Lycos, Yahoo! (a bit different) or others like them – ideally, submit it to all of them.

AltaVista (one of the best) claims, at the time of writing, to have an index of more than 30,000,000 pages, and the site receives twelve million daily requests. However, the server only starts with a few thousand known Web documents, and follows chains of hyperlinks to find all the others. This is achieved by tracking down the links in those documents and indexing them. So, the more documents your Web site is linked to, the more chance you have of getting a 'hit' when someone searches for the subject of your Web page in AltaVista or the others.

Submitting your URL

However, you can add your URL directly to AltaVista – essentially, you are telling them it exists – by getting into the AltaVista home page. At the bottom there is a small, highlighted area which includes 'Add URL'. Click on this, and you will get the electronic form shown in Figure 21.

Make sure your linking is not too recursive – in other words, it is

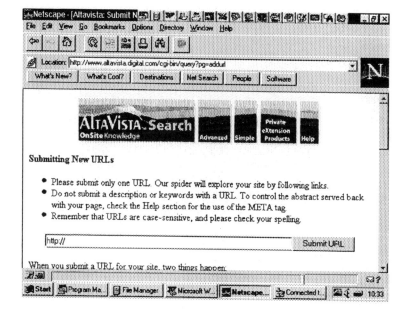

Fig. 21. Submitting your Web page to Alta Vista.

linked to sites which link back to your Web site, but none of these
links go anywhere else. A set of Web documents that link to each
other and have hyperlinks outwards, but that have no hyperlinks
into them from the rest of the Web, cannot be found automatically
by searching programs.

AltaVista uses a spider called Scooter. This Scooter follows all
the links in your Web page and indexes most of your site after a
while.

Excluding pages from the AltaVista index

The AltaVista spider, Scooter, will find any URL connected to the
main body of the Web through even one link. If you don't want your
entire site to be indexed, you can make the Robots Exclusion
Standard ignore some of it by setting up a robots.txt file. This gives
you control over how much of your site is indexed. A typical
robots.txt file looks like this (AltaVista's own example):

```
User-agent:  *           # directed to all
spiders, not just Scooter
```

```
Disallow: /cgi-bin/sources
Disallow: /access_stats
Disallow: /cafeteria/lunch_menus/
```

Type in after the 'Disallow' command any of your nest of Web pages you don't want indexed. The example of lunch menus is a good one. If you were, say, General Motors, you would certainly want everyone in the world accessing your new car information and the like but it's unlikely anybody would want to see what's for lunch in the canteen on any given day. So, you exclude or Disallow it. The spider cannot guarantee that any URL matching one of the disallowed patterns will be ignored by robots visiting your Web site, or that the exclusion will happen immediately, but the robots.txt file is read by Scooter every few days.

When you call up the page shown in Figure 21, you will see the following message or one very like it:

```
Submitting New URLs
Please submit only one URL. Our spider will
explore your site by following links.
Do not submit a description or keywords with a
URL. To control the abstract served back with
your page, check the Help section for the use of
the META tag.
```

Remember that URLs are case-sensitive, and please check your spelling.

When you submit the URL for your Web site to AltaVista, two things happen:

1. Your Home Page is immediately added to the index. It should be available for queries, AltaVista say, in less than a day. This step may fail; for example, if your service provider's server is down or if the network is busy.

2. In any case you will get some sort of status notification when you submit your URL, because AltaVista will immediately try to access it.

Submitting with Submit It!

AltaVista, like many other searchers, accepts submissions of URLs through Scott Banister's Submit It! service (*http://www.submit-it.com/*) for which you will pay. Submit It! claims to allow you to select from up to 200 catalogues and that some of the more popular catalogues on the Web get over 70 per cent of their submissions from Submit It!

Every day the Catalogue Crawler checks every catalogue site for updated or out-of-date submission forms and updates the service. The licences are company-based rather than URL-based so while some Web promotion services charge for submitted, Submit It! charges no extra to submit new URLs. There is a 50 per cent discount for schools, colleges and universities.

NOT ALL SEARCH ENGINES ARE THE SAME

Ever wondered why giving the same search criteria to a variety of search engines will come up with very different ranked listings? Some will put a site at number one that others miss completely. That is because they do not all index Web pages the same way.

Submitting exactly the same search criteria (train spotting Netherlands anorak free) to three of the major search engines to see what they would come up with gave the listings below on a particular day. The top one or two ranked finds are shown in each case. The results were surprisingly disparate and if you want to follow any of the links to Web pages shown here, that's your prerogative. The listing are reproduced 'as is' and any spelling mistakes are in the originals.

AltaVista

UWS Hiking Club Homepage
WELCOME to the UWS Hiking Club Homepage. "Ohhh, this is great ....so stimulating". His breath was accelerating and his body moved rhythmically. "Is
http://www.swan.ac.uk/AU/hiking/home.html - size 3K - 26 Jun 96
http://www.swan.ac.uk/AU/hiking/- size 3K- 6 Jun 96

Personal Details
Personal Details. Age: 22. Weight: 60 kg. Height: 2.01 m. Appearance: There is a portrait of me done by Private Eye showing me train spotting with my...
http://www.dcs.st-and.ac.uk/~mkw/person_details.html - size 492 bytes -17 Jun 96

Netscape (InfoSeek)
The Virtual Anorak
- - http://www.geocities.com/SiliconValley/2276/ (Score 51, Size 7K)
". by Nigel Freeman. Welcome to The Virtual Anorak the site dedicated to all those sad enough to spend their time browsing the Web when they could be out enjoying some healthy exercise and (See also Similar Pages)

ANORAK CENTRAL
- - http://www.hk.super.net/~dbhk/home.html (Score 50, Size 2K)
A Train Spotters Paradise. This is the evolving home page of Darren Breeze, A Videotape Editor with Star TV in Hong Kong, in desperate need of a life!!. You are Visitor number. You Station Master (See also Similar Pages)

Excite
89% Here We Go! - Virtual Reality Football! [Find Similar]
URL:http://www.cee.hw.ac.uk/~ceegha/hwg/virtual.html
Summary: Those of us who refuse to line the pockets of super rich tycoons like Rupert Murdoch to see football on TV have found a free alternative; teletext. As a regular attendee at Hibs matches I dont have to go through the agony of watching the score appearing on a screen as I usually see it happening in front of me, but when we dont have a game teletext comes into its own.

89% Anoraknaphobia!! [Find Similar]
URL:http://www.wadham.ox.ac.uk/~njh/anoraks.html
Summary: They control the technology, they dominate our universities, they read train timetables. Haven't you noticed every other personal homepage has a Star Trek link?

Isn't it amazing what people do with their spare time? Try the same search criteria and you'll no doubt come up with other listings as pages change, move, go away or get abandoned like a Christmas puppy.

Notice also how many of these had clearly put little or no thought into keywords or descriptions, so the indexer simply took the first few lines of body text.

GUIDE TO SEARCH ENGINES

Disappointed that your own 'trainspotting anoraks go to Holland free' Web page didn't even get a mention in these searches? So how can you guarantee that your Web page will get picked up and ranked highly? Here are some pointers to the commonest search engines and how to maximise the impact your Web page will have.

InfoSeek

Infoseek supports both the keywords and description <META> tags. A description can be up to 200 characters (say, 25 words) and the keywords up to 1,000 characters (120 words). If you repeat versions of a keyword more than seven times, InfoSeek will ignore the entire keyword list. This is a guess, but it's probably to get round the problem of idiots putting 'Sex Sex Sex Sex Sex...' hundreds of times as their keywords in the hope that the site will come top of any ranking.

If you do not use a description in a <META> tag, InfoSeek will take the first 200 characters after the <BODY> tag as the description of your Web page. So either make your first 200 words as accurate a description as possible of your Web site (a good idea anyway) or use <META> tags. Do both, in fact.

If your home page has a lot of graphics (it may be entirely graphical), you can describe your page with the ALT attribute in the <IMG> tag, which InfoSeek will index. Remember that the syntax for an <IMG> tag code is:

```
<IMG SRC="/images/haggis.gif" ALT="picture of a
haggis">
```

Excite

At the time of writing, Excite does not make use of tags but generates keywords and summaries automatically. However, all is not lost. Excite's crawler picks up common words or themes in a page and for the summary selects sentences that contain these words or have that general theme. The words in these sentences become the keywords for the site. Avoid ambiguous phrases, particularly at the top of your page. But if there is not enough text the crawler will dig deeper into the site in its search for meaning. Excite prefers a complete, punctuated sentence, just like your old English teacher.

HotBot

HotBot supports both the keywords and description <META> tags. It also has the useful facility that if you search for what you think will absolutely guarantee your Web page a high index ranking, and it doesn't, you can e-mail bugs@hotbot.com, tell them your problem and Web page URL and they'll do their best for you. Nice people.

Lycos

Lycos has a nice, simple crawler. (Simple it may be, but in fact it uses a sophisticated artificial intelligence routine within its crawler, which they call a spider, to generate keywords.) It looks at the text of your Web page and makes up a title and description from this. It selects a bit of the Web site that represents the overall theme and displays this as the description. The Lycos spider may be bright, but it doesn't like pictures. Do not start your page with an image map or Lycos will not make an abstract for your HTML page.

WebCrawler

WebCrawler looks at the <TITLE> tag for the name of your Web page. Other search engines will make up a summary from the <BODY> text of your document but WebCrawler will use the URL if you don't include a title.

Yahoo!

Yahoo! is the grandaddy of Web searchers and is a law unto itself. It is not so much a search engine as a directory but different from other directories in that you could find yourself listed on Yahoo! without submitting your Web page URL. This is because Yahoo! has a crawler (they call it a robot) that searches for new Web sites at certain places on the Internet (announcement sites, cool sites and so on) on the basis that anything new will get to these places at some point in time. However, Yahoo! say that most of their new listings come via Web pages being manually added using the Yahoo! 'Add URL' submission form. Yahoo! doesn't allow keyword suggestion on the 'Add URL' form but takes keywords from the document text, the name you give your listing, and a comments field (in which you have 15–20 words to say it all).

GETTING THE TOP RANKINGS

Use keywords in your HTML document

Make these as descriptive as possible, if you want people honestly to know what your Web page is about. 'Steam train fanatics look here' will get more interest that 'Trains – general interest'. If all you want is lots of people visiting, a typical con trick is to include a string of obscene language since pornography-related searches are amongst the commonest, sadly, on the Web.

Use a descriptive title

The crawler which accesses your site for indexing will look first at the <TITLE> tag (not the first HTML heading on your page) and this is what a Web browser will display in its title bar. Search engines will show this text located between the <TITLE> tags when your Web page comes up in a search list. Those sites which have no titles, only key words, are deplorable largely because when you add the page to your Bookmark and go to look for it later you will find it hard to remember what the document was about.

Use <META> tags

<META> tags let you give more detail about your Web pages which determines how your pages are indexed (not that all search engines make use of <META> tags).

USING THE <META> TAG

<META> tag codes go between the <HEAD> - - - - - - <HEAD> tag. Your HTML editor or Web authoring tool, if you use one, may allow you to mark a line as META, but if you are writing HTML pages from scratch, the syntax is:

```
<META name="description" content="train spot-
ters meet in Rhyl">.
```

This will appear after the title in an index listing.

Keywords

Alternatively, you could use meaningful keywords in <META>, such as:

```
<META name="keywords" content="trains, train-
spotting, anorak, Rhyl, railways">
```

This is not seen by the reader of your page but is meat and drink to the search engine crawler and indexer. A lot of sites still do not include <META> tags and in any case the crawler is going to make an index list from every single word in your document. Therefore use keywords that may not appear in the main text of your Web page. 'Train' and 'Train-spotters' may be redundant in your <META> tag since they are in the title. But one good use of keywords is to give alternative spelling or usages, such as 'train-spotter, train spotter, train-spotters, train spotters, Train-spotter, Train Spotter, Train-spotting, Train Spotting' and so on.

<META> **tags in frames**

If you have frames in your Web page, the main HTML file will contain a <FRAMESET> tag. This may not give a crawler much in the way of useful information when trying to make an abstract, so include a summary of the contents of the frames on your page with <META> tags.

<META> **tags in JavaScript at the top of the page**

Crawlers, being simple beasts, take more account of text at the top of the page than the dross nearer the bottom. JavaScript code, if you use it, will probably take up the first few hundred characters on your HTML page, so use <META> tags to describe your page.

Mix and match

You can have as many <META> lines as you wish, so mix and match any or all of the above ideas to get your Web page indexed and noticed.

Netscape Editor makes it easy for you with Properties Document which provides a menu in which you can add <META> tags in the General and/or Advanced areas. Try adding to these and checking the result in the browser and in the HTML source.

UNDERSTANDING DIRECTORIES

Directories are constructed just like the File Manager or Windows Explorer you probably use – they are hierarchical databases. You probably have your files and programs in a few major directories or folders and within each one there are sub-directories or sub-folders and inside them, files. A program like Winword.exe might be inside Programs/MSOffice/MSapps/Winword, for instance.

Net directories are organised by subject. This would suggest to the naive observer that choosing the right subject category would be the most important aspect to submitting your Web site to the directory. That's partly true. You do need to think about the best category or categories to put your URL into. Then people interested in that subject will stand a greater chance of finding your Web site. But, and it's a big but, this gets tricky when each directory has a different set of categories and sub-categories.

There is no magic formula and no single answer to getting your Web site listed in all directories and guides, but try some or all of these tips.

Choosing your categories

- Don't pick a category because it looks relatively empty. There's probably a good reason for that. Better to choose one that is full to bursting. It's likely to be popular.

- That said, don't choose a category that is full but too general.

- Look for organisations or services most like yours, see where they are listed and follow the herd.

- You cannot guarantee that a category like Leisure or Nature means the same in every directory.

- If you can't find an appropriate category, try suggesting a new one to the Site administrators.

- You cannot automatically enter your Web site into a Cool Link category. Try it and you'll probably get a raspberry e-mail back for your cheek. The SysOps pick them, not us mortals.

- Web directory organisers have neat, tidy minds. They also don't want Web users confused between what is a business (selling something) and a personal home page (telling something).

- Usually, a business Web page link must be put in a Business category. Choose the best two or three (the maximum you're likely to be allowed). Personal pages will have an appropriate category to go into.

Using good descriptions and names

- Both title and comments fields should have good descriptions of your company, service or interest, as outlined above. Ideally, your Web site address should be descriptive too, but most people can't control that since they are on a large service provider's server.

- If you have your own Web server, make its name meaningful (Diamonds.uk.com for instance, if you buy and sell diamonds).

- There is a debate as to whether abbreviated company names are a good idea. The argument goes that if you sell machines to businesses internationally you should list yourself as International Business Machines. But you'll notice that IBM doesn't. It's probably to do with recognition. What does BAM sell? No idea, but if they'd called themselves British Aqualung Manufacturers you might have bought your next scuba diving kit from them.

- Ever wonder why so many mini-cab firms are called AAA Cabs or 123 Cabs? So they can get listed first in the phone book and get picked out. By all means do it in the phone book but don't bother on the Web – most search engines know that trick.

Notifying any changes

- If you change your URL (say you sign up with a different server) resubmit the Web page. The search engine crawler will visit the old site, not find your URL and drop it.

- But even if you change or update your Web pages a lot you may not need to resubmit, as the crawler will find the updates and re-index them. Resubmitting will speed this up a bit, although it's a pain to go through it all again with every directory.

- Some tricky people change the title (in the <TITLE> tag) of the Web page regularly in the hope that search engines will think it's a new site and add it to the existing description, thus increasing the find rate. It's very naughty.

- So is putting yards of junk keywords somewhere (usually at the top or bottom) of the HTML document in the hope that if a crawler sees the word 'free' or 'windows' a hundred times it will give the site a high rating. As mentioned previously, some crawlers know about this and exclude any word with more than a given number of appearances.

- Keep a list of all the directories, search engines and guides you submit to. You'll be amazed how quickly you forget. Keep it in a simple Notepad text file (mylists.txt) and cut single lines from this file and paste them into the URL box at the top left of Netscape. This will take you instantly to that directory. Alternatively, keep them in your browser's Bookmarks listing.

KNOWING THE TOP 100 SITES FOR LINKING

Would you like to guarantee that you know the best sites to send your links to? John Audette of the Multimedia Marketing Group has done a lot of the work for you. He maintains a free on-line database of what he considers to be the top 100 places to register a Web site free. webStep TOP 100 contains annotations and links directly to the registration pages of listed sites. It also lists the most important sites to register with (in his opinion) called Elite 30 on the basis that you'll get 80 per cent of the results from 20 per cent of the sites. Visit the TOP 100 at: *http://www.mmgco.com/top100.html*. The e-mail address is ja@mmgco.com.

13
Uploading Your Web Page

YOU CAN DO IT!

You can now design a proper Web site. Please start by making a new subdirectory in the C drive, called 'newweb' or some other suitable name (C:\newweb) with its own subdirectories C:\newweb\development and C:\newweb\images. You will develop your pages in one subdirectory and your images in another, moving the finished versions to \newweb when they are ready. The reasons for this are twofold:

1. When you come to upload your own Web pages to a service provider, the server may not be able to handle a directory structure and all relevant HTML documents and images will have to be in one directory.

2. However, you are bound to lose track of what the finished versions are or want to alter them. Earlier and in-development files in subdirectories keeps the whole process tidier.

But how do you get your Web pages on to a server so the world can see them?

ASK YOUR ISP

With any luck, you will have signed up with an Internet Service Provider who will offer you 5 or 10MB free space for your web site. Or you may be able to load it on to a server at your work. Alternatively, you can rent space from a space provider.

Once your Web pages are designed and working they have to be uploaded to the server for these to work. Only your Internet Service Provider can give you instructions about how to upload your pages. In some cases it can be done semi-automatically (you just indicate what the files are called and they get sent to the server's computer) and in others you may have to post them, by mail, on a disk. Some ISPs make it very easy:

- if you are signed up with the Microsoft Network (*http://www.microsoft.com*), you will be provided with a set of tools called Web Publisher (or Microsoft Web Publishing Wizard, WPW) to do most of it for you

- if you have another service like Compuserve or AOL they will have similar routines

- if your employer is your ISP (at a college or large company, for example) ask the appropriate department what to do.

In all cases, check the documentation you got from your ISP. You may have to access their Web site to download whatever software you need.

NETLOAD

For more experienced users, there is a general utility called NetLoad (available at *http://www.aerosoft.com.au/netLoad* e-mail: *andrew@aerosoft.com.au*) which can automate the process. You will need to get upload codes from whoever runs your server – ask them for details.

WEBDRIVE

Another useful utility, WebDrive, lets you deal with your remote server site as if it were an extra disk drive on your own PC. Contact *http:/www.riverfrontsoftware.com*

14
Getting Listed

AFTER THE WEB PAGE – WHAT NEXT?

Your Web page is up and running and you hope people are going to look at it. What then?

YOU KNOW WHO YOU ARE – HOW DOES ANYONE ELSE?

An accusation often levelled at the Net and the Web is that there is no way to find anyone's e-mail address. Not true, but it does depend on them having put it into a directory of some sort. There are a number of these; for example WhoWhere, Four/1, IAT, Bigfoot and Switchboard). See Figure 22 – this page came from *http:// home.netscape.com/home/internet-white-pages.html*.

There are many other 'white pages' directories as well, mostly offering a free listing and searching service. Incidentally, we are used to the concept of *Yellow Pages* in the UK but not 'White Pages', which is what Americans have always called the non-classified section of the phone book.

GETTING OTHERS TO DO THE WORK

Electronic classified advertisement distributors exist. You pay to have your advert and information placed in a sort of electronic yellow pages along with many others. The lists are organised by classification. This is posted in various places – certain of the big, well-travelled Web sites, popular on-line services, bulletin boards – and sent to people who request such listings on a regular basis. This can be quite cheap and fairly effective.

Often you can get one to three months free if you book for a longer period, or as a trial. Look on any of the main pages associated with Web searchers such as Lycos, AltaVista, Magellan, etc. and see who is advertising and what. They will generally have a

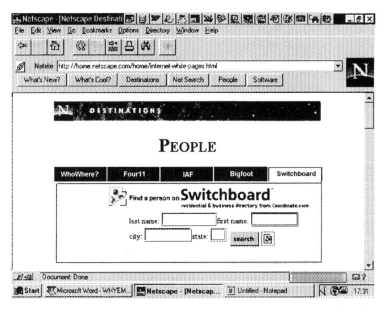

Fig. 22. Listing yourself in a Directory is a good way to get noticed.

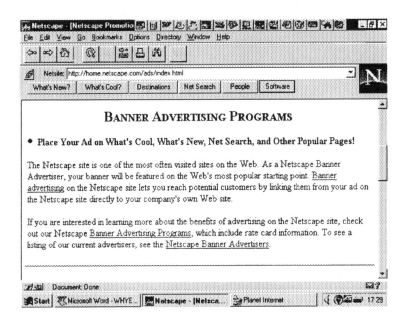

Fig. 23. Banner advertising – if you can afford it, do it.

'Click here for further information' button which will download for you a description of the service.

Banner advertising

If you want to go the whole hog with a banner advertising campaign in Netscape or any of the other well-visited pages, Figure 23 is an illustration and URL of where you can start. One of the great advantages of using Web advertising over straightforward e-mail is the ability to build into your Web page access to video, sound, real graphics, etc. which anyone with the appropriate plug-ins can receive.

Usenet advertising

Some Usenet newsgroups allow and encourage advertising on the basis that people do want to know what's on offer, and in some cases it can make money for the Usenet. Usually this is no more than a pointer to an auto-responder e-mail address. There are a few newsgroups that allow commercial advertising. Have a look at alt.business.misc for an example of this (see Figure 24.)

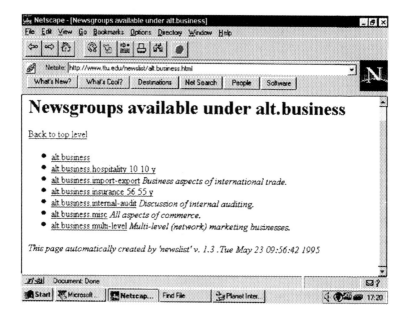

Fig. 24. Usenet advertising – but check which news groups allow it.

DOES INTERACTIVE ADVERTISING WORK?

Does a car work? Depends on the car. Netscape, AT&T, InfoSeek and ABC recently commissioned a survey of media buyers, the people in advertising agencies who buy space on behalf of clients. The survey concentrated on those actively involved in interactive advertising, so it's not exactly an unbiased survey and you'd hardly expect Netscape to tell us if the results were less than glowing, but none the less it makes interesting reading. Here, according to Netscape, are the highlights:

> Advertisers say that they use their own Web sites to deliver product information, establish corporate identity, build brand awareness and loyalty, capture customer leads, provide customer service, conduct sales transactions and conduct research. To complete the marketing mix, they use print ads, direct mail and directories to guide people to their sites.

> Advertisers plan to increase dramatically their spending on interactive media this year, reporting that their 1996 budgets for interactive media were from 50 per cent to more than 200 percent higher than in 1995.

So there you are.

Advertising with commercial on-line services
If you use Compuserve, AOL, etc. as your service provider you will have seen ads in the classified areas and related forums of the commercial on-line services and on start-up. You pay for this, and your service provider will be only too delighted to tell you how much.

Don't forget the papers
Not everyone is Netted or Webbed. Don't ignore the more conventional classified advertisement routes such as print and TV, if you can afford it. But include your Web page and e-mail addresses in there. On the other hand, it probably doesn't cost much for a couple of lines in *Train Spotters' Monthly* or whatever publication which is, you can bet, read cover to cover by all train spotters. If you have an e-mail address they'll all be diving for their keyboards the minute they put down the magazine. The same goes for other special interest publications. But make sure you have something real to offer.

15
Twenty Top Tips for Webbers

Keep it simple, stupid

This is the KISS principle. Keep your Web pages simple, straightforward, full of 'what's in it for you, the customer' information and easy-to-read. Don't forget (yes, some people do) to include a short description of what you do, your Web address, e-mail address and auto-responder post-box if any, so that people can send messages to and automatically receive information about your shared interests, products or services.

Keep it interactive

Make them do something. Have a call-to-action somewhere on your Web pages, even if it's only 'Type in your name and e-mail address' posted by a form to your e-mail address. Great way to start your own member or customer list!

Keep it relevant

Remember who's paying – the viewers, through their phone bill and connect charges. The Web is accessed by millions of people every day; and potentially everyone is your customer or contact. Before you begin to create your site, identify your target audience and write your site based on what you would want to see if you were in their shoes.

Keep it general

Don't make your Web page browser-specific. You may be in love with Internet Explorer or some other browser, but Netscape on a 12-inch monitor with a slow graphics card might display pages in a different way. Test your pages by getting friends with other browsers and hardware to look at them and comment on design, speed of download, accessibility, legibility, colour clashes, etc.

Keep it tidy

Work out your Web page design before you start writing any text.

Don't just lay a design over a converted text page – Web publishing is not text publishing with knobs on.

Keep it fast

There is no better way to slow down a Web page than having a complicated, large graphic right at the top. What's more, this may stop some indexers accessing it. Use the LOWSRC trick and interlaced GIFs and keep graphics simple, small and light. If you must have big, 16.7 million-colour photographs (for instance, if you are running a slide library or a tourist attraction) put these in other pages and provide links to them from a thumbnail.

Keep it organised

Think very carefully before sticking a long, long document in as a Web page. Break it up into a series of linked HTML documents with good navigation between them. Alternatively, add a table of contents at the top with links to other sections. Better still, put the contents up as a Web page and offer the whole document as a download.

Keep it top-heavy

Don't put the good stuff at the very bottom of your Web page, like the final solution to a mystery novel. Most viewers won't get that far.

Keep it polite

If anyone e-mails you, reply, even if it's only a 'Thank you for your message' message. A group e-mail takes no more time (and money) to send than a single one.

Keep promoting it (I)

Paper has not gone out of fashion. If you're in business, add your Web site and e-mail addresses to your letterhead, fax cover sheets, business cards, other ads, posters, leaflets and fliers.

Keep promoting it (II)

On the other hand, paper is going out of fashion. Let other Webbers know you exist – register with search engines, post messages in relevant newsgroups, get on public e-mail lists (LISTSERVs) and announce yourself in *comp.infosystems.www.announce*

Keep promoting it (III)

There are lots of on-line E-zines and if you can find one relevant to your interests, make an announcement. John Labovitz maintains a list of over 800 E-zines with a keyword search at *http: www.meer.net/ ~john1/e-zine-list/index.html*

Keep it linked

Use the Web's talent for hypertext and hypermedia to its fullest advantage. Apart from making sure your Web site is linked by the various browsers, search engines and directories, get other companies you see advertising to swap links with you. If the customers are buying your shoes, chewing gum, financial services and the like, chances are they're interested in other people's. And that cuts both ways.

Keep giving away information

Web surfers love a freebie and free info, if it is really free and really is informative, will keep people coming to your site, which also means...

Keep changing it

Updating daily or every few days is essential. There is nothing more depressing than a Web site whose last update was six months ago. Why go back to it?

Keep it interesting

Even big companies put out boring and dull Web sites, using graphics and text they wouldn't let out of the door as a handbill. Why? Because they haven't realised the potential yet. Get one step ahead and entertain the viewer.

Keep your focus

The Web is not all. Using The Web should only be part of your marketing. Don't forget newsgroups, Usenets and mailing lists. Be cunning and you can get your message through in a few lines of Sig file, even if straight ads are discouraged.

Keep your head

Don't worry about the technology. You do *not* have to be a computer genius to do any of this. If you really can't manage any of it, get someone in who can – neighbours' kids, placement students from the local college, NetNerds on the dole, the denizens of your local Internet Café, boy scouts, the lucky people who sold you all this stuff – there are lots of people who'd love to get their hands on some new (free) kit and show off.

Keep at it

Your first Web site will be *dreadful* just like everybody else's. One of the nice things about the wonderfully helpful Netizen community is that if they don't like your site, they'll tell you so! Listen. You can change it as often as you like.

Keep at it

Keep improving, keep testing, keep developing, keep updating, keep asking people what they think, keep listening, keep responding and above all...keep your sense of humour.

And as E. M. Forster said: '**Only connect**'.

Appendix
HTML Tag Summary

This Appendix summarises the tags allowed in HTML 3.0 at the time of writing. Not all these tags are supported by all browsers, but this changes almost daily as new browser versions emerge with more and more properties. Therefore, very little information is included as to which tags are supported by which browsers as this will probably be out of date. Consult the help file for your browser or any browser you want your Web page to be seen by.

Tag, attribute or value	Description
< ! - - . . .	Comments ignored by the browser. Put these before < HTML >.
<!DOCTYPE ..>	Specifies the Document Type Identifier (DTD) – the HTML standard and level of your document. Put these before < HTML >.
<A ...>...</A>	Anchor-marked text for a hypertext link or bookmark. NAME or HREF attribute required.
...HREF	Makes all text a hyperlink. HREF= "#place" refers to an anchor called "place" within the same document.
Mailto : ...	Opens e-mail dialogue box and sends e-mail.
...NAME	Makes the anchor a bookmark (target of a link).
...TITLE	Title of document linked to (for information only).
... REL	Used with HREF, gives the list of relationships between anchor and targets.

...REV	Used with HREF, gives the list of relationships between target and anchor.
...METHODS	Tells the user what can be done with or to the linked object (information only).
...TARGET	When clicked, the browser will open a new window called the TARGET name.
</ADDRESS>...<ADDRESS>	Markup tag, useful when providing an address.
<APPLET>...</APPLET>	Executes a pre-written Java script (an Applet).
...ALIGN	How the applet display is aligned – left, right, top, texttop, middle, abs-middle, baseline, bottom, absbottom.
...ALT	Alternative text if the applet can't be run.
...CODE	The file containing the Java applet.
...CODEBASE	The base URL of the Java applet – the directory where it exists.
...HSPACE	Pixels on each side of the applet display.
...NAME	Specifies a name for the applet.
...PARAM NAME=	Specifies an applet-specific attribute.
...PARAM VALUE=	Specifies an applet-specific attribute.
...VSPACE	Pixels above the applet display.
...WIDTH/HEIGHT	Size in pixels of the applet's display.
<B>...</B>	Boldtext.
<BASE HREF=...>	The URL of the document (put within </HEAD>...</HEAD>).
...TARGET	Default target window when these are not specified in links.
<BASEFONT SIZE=>	Size of the standard font. Default is 3, range 1–7.
...FACE	Changes the typeface of the Basefont.
...COLOR	Changes the colour of the Basefont.

`<BGSOUND SRC=. . .>`	In-line sound (.WAV, .AU or .MID) for Internet Explorer.
`. . .LOOP=n`	Number of times to play file. Use LOOP = -1 or LOOP = INFINITE to play constantly.
`. . .DELAY=n`	Delay start by n seconds.
`<BIG>. . .</BIG>`	Puts text in a bigger font.
`</BLINK>. . .</BLINK>`	Blinking text.
`<BLOCKQUOTE>. . .</BLOCKQUOTE>`	
	Text quoted from another source. Puts in a paragraph break.
`<BODY. . .>. . .</BODY>`	All the text and images in a page.
`. . .BACKGROUND=`	Filename of background image.
`. . .TEXT="#RRGGBB"/"colourname"`	
	Colour of text.
`. . .LINK=`	Colour of link text.
`. . .VLINK=`	Colour of link text when visited.
`. . .ALINK=`	Colour of link text when active.
`. . .BGCOLOR=`	Background colour.
`. . .BGPROPERTIES=FIXED`	Background image does not scroll.
`. . .LEFTMARGIN="n"`	Indents document by n pixels.
`. . .TOPMARGIN`	Document has n pixels top margin.
` `	Line break.
`. . .CLEAR="LEFT/RIGHT/ALL"`	
	Line break and move down until left, right or both margins are clear.
`<CAPTION>. . .</CAPTION>`	Caption for a table.
`. . .ALIGN="top/bottom/left/right/center"`	
	Aligns caption relative to the table.
`. . .VALIGN="top/bottom"`	Aligns caption relative to the table.
`<CENTER>. . .</CENTER>`	Centres text between margins.
`<CITE>. . .</CITE>`	Marks text as a citation or reference.
`<CODE>. . .</CODE>`	Indicates a piece of computer code (usually in a non-proportional font).
`<COL>`	Text alignment for table columns.

```
...ALIGN="center/left/right/justify"
```
Text alignment within a column. Center is default.

```
...SPAN="n"
```
Number of columns to which **ALIGN** refers.

```
...VALIGN="baselinetop/middle/bottom"
```
Text alignment within a column. Bottom is default.

`<COLGROUP>...</COLGROUP>` Groups columns so that **ALIGN**, **SPAN** and **VALIGN** refer to them all.

```
...SPAN="n"
```
Number of columns to which **ALIGN** refers.

```
...ALIGN="center/left/right/justify"
```
Text alignment within a column group. Center is default.

```
...VALIGN="baselinetop/middle/bottom"
```
Text alignment within a column group. Bottom is default.

`<COMMENT>...</COMMENT>` Text will not appear on-screen.

`<DFN>...</DFN>` A 'defining instance' of a term (such as the first time it is used).

`<DIR>...</DIR>` Directory list (no bullet). Listed elements start with < LI >.

`<DIV ALIGN="left/right/center">...</DIV>` All text within a division will be formatted the same way.

`<DL>...</DL>` Definition list.

`<DT>` Definition term.

`<DD>` Definition.

`... COMPACT` Makes the whole list a compact style.

`<EM>...</EM>` Emphasises text.

`<EMBED SRC=".">` Embeds a document, image or other file exactly as it appears in its native application. Use in Netscape for audio and video.

`...LOOP=n` Number of times to play file. Use LOOP=-1 or LOOP=INFINITE to play constantly.

`...DELAY=n`	Delay start by *n* seconds.
`<FONT ...>...</FONT>`	
`..SIZE=n`	Size of the font. Default is 3, range 1–7.
`..COLOR="#rrggbb" or ="#colourname"`	
	Changes the colour of the font.
`..FACE=`	Changes the typeface of the font.
`<FOR>...</FORM>`	Surrounds a data input form.
`ACTION=`	The URL to which the form information is sent.
`METHOD="GET/POST"`	Specifies what happens to the form information.
`<FRAMESET...>...</FRAMESET>`	
	Surrounds frame information. Replaces < BODY >.
`...ROWS="n"`	Height of rows in FRAMESET (pixels).
`...COLS="n"`	Width of columns in FRAMESET (pixels).
`<FRAME...>`	Sets up a single frame within a FRAMESET.
`...SRC=`	URL of file to be shown in frame.
`...NAME=`	Gives a frame a name.
`...MARGINWIDTH="n"`	Space (pixels) between frame sides and contents.
`...MARGINHEIGHT="n"`	Space (pixels) between frame top/bottom and contents.
`...SCROLLING="yes/no/auto"`	
	Determines whether frame has a scrollbar.
`...NORESIZE`	Does not allow viewer to resize frame.
`...FRAMEBORDER="yes/no"`	Sets display of frame border.
`...FRAMESPACING="n"`	Sets space (pixels) around a frame.
`<Hn ALIGN="left/right /center"...>`	
	Aligns text within a Heading style (H1–H6).

`<HEAD>...</HEAD>`	Information about the HTML document. *Must* contain <TITLE>. Can include <BASE> and <ISINDEX> <LINK>, <META> and <NEXTID>.
`<HR...>`	Horizontal rule (line).
`...SIZE=n`	Rule thickness (pixels).
`...WIDTH=n/x%`	Width of rule in pixels (*n*) or percentage of page width (*x*%).
`...ALIGN=left/right/center`	Aligns rule on page.
`...NOSHADE`	Provides a solid (unshaded) rule.
`...COLOR=name/#rrggbb`	Sets colour of rule.
`<HTML>...</HTML>`	Identifies an HTML document. Must immediately follow the prologue identifier <!DOCYTPE...>.
`<I>...</I>`	Italic text.
`<IMG ...>`	Sets an in-line graphic.
`...ALIGN=left/right/top/middle/bottom/texttop/absmiddle/absbottombaseline/`	Aligns the image and any surrounding text.
`...ALT="Text"`	Alternative text is image cannot be viewed.
`...ISMAP`	Identifies image as a server-side image map (used in clickable graphics).
`...SRC="..."`	URL of the image.
`...WIDTH=w`	Width of image (pixels).
`...HEIGHT=h`	Height of image (pixels).
`...BORDER=b`	Width of image border. Do not use =0.
`...VSPACE=v`	Space above and below an image (pixels).
`...HSPACE=h`	Space left and right of an image (pixels).
`...LOWSRC="..."`	Use alongside SRC="..." to specify a low resolution image to load first. This can speed up loading.

`...USEMAP`	Identifies image as a client-side image map (used in clickable graphics).
`...VRML="..." HEIGHT=h WIDTH=w`	Specifies an in-line animated VRML world. Pane size can be set (pixels).
`<INPUT...>`	An input text field (contents can be edited by viewer).
`..ALIGN=left/right/top/middle/bottom/texttop/` `absmiddle/absbottombaseline/`	Vertical alignment of the INPUT field and any associated text.
`...CHECKED`	Checkbox or radio button selected by default.
`...MAXLENGTH="m"`	Maximum number of characters that can be typed into the INPUT field. If larger than SIZE, the field contents will scroll.
`...NAME="..."`	Unique name you give to the form field's contents.
`...SIZE="s"`	Visible width of the field (characters).
`...SRC="..."`	URL of an image in a field.
`...TYPE="CHECKBOX/HIDDEN/IMAGE/PASSWORD/RADIO/` `RESET/SUBMIT/TEXT/TEXTAREA/FILE"`	Sets the type of input the field will accept and display. Default in TEXT.
`...VALUE`	Sets the initial value of an input field (if numbers or text) or the value returned when the field is selected. This is required for radio buttons.
`<ISINDEX ...>`	Tells browser document may be searched by key words.
`...ACTION="..."`	Specifies URL of program or cgi script the search text will be passed to.
`...PROMPT="..."`	Text to replace the default prompt text.
`<KBD>...</KBD>`	Typeface to indicate text to be typed by a viewer.
`<LI>`	Lines in MENU, UL, OL lists.

`<LINK>`	Indicates a link to another document. Takes same syntax and attributes as `<A>` but without a closing tag.
`<LISTING>`	Displays text as fixed-width (like `<PRE>`) and may translate special characters.
`<MAP NAME="mapname">`	Names a map so that it can be referenced by an image statement `<IMG...>`.
`...AREA`	Describes each AREA in a clickable MAP.
`...SHAPE="shape"`	Shape of a MAP AREA. The first SHAPE which appears lies on 'top' of other regions if they overlap.
`...COORDS="x,y"`	Coordinates of a MAP AREA.
`...HREF="result.html">`	Defines the document linked when the AREA is clicked.
`...NOHREF`	Clicking on a NOHREF area has no result (this is the default).
`<MARQUEE>...>...</MARQUEE>`	Creates scrolling Marquee text in Internet Explorer.
`...ALIGN=TOP/MIDDLE/BOTTOM`	Aligns text with marquee.
`...BEHAVIOR=SCROLL/SLIDE/ALTERNATE`	Text will scroll continuously, scroll and stop or move back and forward in the marquee.
`...BGCOLOR="#rrggbb/#colourname"`	Sets colour for marquee background.
`...DIRECTION=left/right`	Sets direction of scroll (left is default).
`...HEIGHT=h/x%`	Height of marquee in pixels (h or percentage of screen ($x\%$).
`...WIDTH=w/y%`	Width of marquee in pixels (w) or percentage of screen ($y\%$).
`...HSPACE=s`	Leaves left and right margins of s pixels.

`...LOOP=n`	Determines how many times the text will scroll. If $l = -1$ or INFINITE, the text will scroll forever.
`...SCROLLAMOUNT=z`	Puts z pixels between one scroll event and the next.
`...SCROLLDELAY=d`	Leaves z milliseconds between one scroll event and the next.
`...VSPACE=v`	Leaves space above and below the marquee (pixels).
`<MENU>...</MENU>`	Displays a list with one element per line (no bullet, more compact than <UL>).
`<META>`	Used within <HEAD>...</HEAD>, this embeds non-display document information for identification, indexing and searching.
`...HTTP-EQUIV="..."`	Generates a response header. Examples are "Expires", "Reply", "Keywords".
`...NAME`	A meta-information name for the document.
`...CONTENT`	Meta-information text associated with NAME or HTTP-EQUIV.
`<NEXTID N="xxxx">`	A unique identifier for the document read by text editors (not HTML browsers).
`<NOBR>...</NOBR>`	Prevents line breaks in a block of text.
`<NOFRAMES>...</NOFRAMES>`	Surrounds alternate content for non-frame-capable browsers.
`<OBJECT>`	Like <IMG...>, a way of inserting an object into Internet Explorer. Like <IMG>, this tag can use HEIGHT, WIDTH, ALIGN BORDER, HSPACE, VSPACE, etc. attributes.
`<PARAM NAME="..." VALUE="...">`	Sets the properties of an object.
`<OL...>...</OL>`	Ordered list (numbered). Individual list lines start with <LI>.

`...TYPE=1/A/a/I/i/`	The list can be numbered with numerals, capital letters, small letters, large Roman numerals or small Roman numerals.
`...START=s`	Starts at a number other than 1 (or A).
`... VALUE=v`	Gives that value to a list item. TYPE and VALUE can be used differently in each < LI >.
`<OPTION DISABLED/SELECTED>`	An option within < SELECT > and its initial properties. < OPTION > elements can be separated along one line or be in a list.
`<P>`	Provides a line break and line space.
`...ALIGN=left/right/center`	Aligns the paragraph text (left is default).
`<PLAINTEXT>...(</PLAINTEXT>)`	Formatted text. Do not use </PLAINTEXT > in Netscape.
`<PRE WIDTH="c">`	Preformatted (fixed-width) text. WIDTH is optional and is in characters, but only 40, 80 and 132 are supported (80 is default).
`<S>...</S>`	Text is ~~struck through~~ (Mosaic). Use < STRIKE > by preference.
`<SAMP>`	Literal characters (fixed-width font).
`<SCRIPT...>...</SCRIPT>`	Embeds a Java (Netscape) or Visual Basic (Internet Explorer) script in a document.
`...LANGUAGE="JavaScript"/"VBS"`	Defines the Script language.
`...SRC="..."`	The URL of the document or program containing the script.
`<SELECT>...</SELECT>`	Allows choice of a set of < OPTION > elements.
`...MULTIPLE`	Allows viewers to make several selections.

`...SIZE="s"`	Sets the number of item lines displayed.
`...NAME=".."`	Sets a name to be submitted when submitting data.
`<SMALL>`	Sets a small font.
`<SOUND ..>`	Plays .WAV files in Mosaic.
`...SRC="soundfil.wav)`	Specifies the sound file to be played.
`...DELAY=d`	Delay in seconds.
`...LOOP=n`	Number of plays (can be = INFINITE).
`<STRIKE>...</STRIKE>`	Displays text as ~~struck through~~.
`<STRONG>...</STRONG>`	Strong emphasis (usually bold).
`<SUB>...</SUB>`	Subscript text.
`<SUP>...</SUP>`	Superscript text.
`<TABLE...>...</TABLE>`	Surrounds table elements.
`...BORDER=b`	Width of table border – can be = 0 (pixels).
`...CELLSPACING=s`	Space between cells in a table – can be = 0 (pixels).
`...CELLPADDING=p`	Margin around text in a cell – can be = 0 (pixels).
`...WIDTH=w/y%`	Width of a table cell in pixels or percentage of display width.
`...HEIGHT=h/x%`	Height of a table cell in pixels or percentage of display width.
`...ALIGN=left/right`	Alignment of a table on the page.
`...VALIGN=top/center/bottom`	Aligns text within a table cell.
`...BGCOLOR="#rrggbb"/"#colorname"`	Assigns a background colour to a table.
`...BORDERCOLOR="#rrggbb"/"#colorname"`	Assigns a colour to the table border (needs BORDER in <TABLE...>).
`...BORDERCOLORLIGHT="#rrggbb"/#colorname"`	Sets a lighter colour on a table border (needs BORDER in <TABLE...>).

`...BORDERCOLORDARK="#rrggbb"/"#colorname"`
Sets a darker colour on a table border (needs **BORDER** in <TABLE...>).

`...BACKGROUND="image.gif"`
Sets an image within a table cell or whole table (Internet Explorer).

`...FRAME=void/above/below/hsides/lhs/rhs/vsides/box`
Displays certain outside borders only (Internet Explorer).

`...RULES=none/basic/rows/cols/all`
Displays certain internal lines (rules) (Internet Explorer).

`<TBODY>`
Specifies the format of the main body of the table – required for **RULES** (Internet Explorer).

`<TD...>`
Table data – sets up a data cell within a table row.

`...ROWSPAN=r`
Specifies how many rows a cell will span.

`...COLSPAN=c`
Specifies how many columns a cell will span.

`...ALIGN=left/center/right`
Aligns text within a table or table cell.

`...VALIGN=top/middle/bottom/baseline`
Aligns text within a table or table cell.

`...WIDTH=w/y%`
Sets the cell width in pixels or as a percentage of the table width.

`...HEIGHT=h/x%`
Sets the cell height in pixels or as a percentage of the table height.

`...NOWRAP`
Prevents text wrapping in a cell.

`...BGCOLOR="#rrggbb"/"#colorname"`
Assigns a background colour to a table cell.

`...BORDERCOLOR="#rrggbb"/"#colorname"` Assigns a colour to the table cell border (needs BOR-DER in <TABLE...>).

`<TFOOT>`
Sets the footer for the table and is not displayed (Internet Explorer).

`<TH...>`	Table header – identical to `<TD>` except that text is in bold. Uses the same attributes as `<TD>`.
`<THEAD>`	Sets the header for the Table and is not displayed (Internet Explorer).
`<TR...>`	Table row – the number of rows is set by the number of separate `<TH>` or `<TD>` cells are described. All the same attributes as `<TD>` can be used.
`<TEXTAREA...>...</TEXTAREA>`	
	An input area that can accept more than one line of input text (unlike `<INPUT>`).
`...NAME="..."`	Sets a name for the text area, useful if linking or submitting.
`...ROWS=r`	Specifies the visible area of the input, in rows of fixed-width font.
`...COLS=c`	Specifies the width of the visible area, in characters of fixed-width font.
`...WRAP=off/virtual/physical`	
	Word wrapping can be OFF (no wrapping and lines sent as typed), VIRTUAL (wraps displayed but text sent as one unbroken string) or PHYSICAL (wrapped, sent as displayed) (Netscape).
`<TITLE>...</TITLE>`	Identifies contents of a document. Required in `<HEAD>...</HEAD>`.
`<TT>`	TeleType – fixed-width typewriter font.
`<U>...</U>`	Underlines text.
`<UL TYPE=disc/circle/square>...</UL>`	
	Unordered list (bulleted). Each list item must be preceded with `<LI>`.
`<VAR>`	Indicates a variable (as in an equation) which displays as italic.
`<WBR>`	Word break – tells a browser where break is allowed if needed.

<XMP>   Displays text in fixed-width font but
with line spaces separating it from
other text and with 80 characters per
line. It may translate special characters.

Glossary

AltaVista. The best Web search tool.

anchor. An HTML tag that can act as a link to another location, or as a bookmark for a link.

AOL. America On Line – the world's largest on-line service provider.

applet. A small independent piece of programming code for a specific function. Soon, a word processor may not be a single, large program on an individual's PC but a conglomeration of applets (for text entry, spelling checking, etc.) that will be called down from elsewhere exactly as needed. Nothing to do with Apple.

Archie. A database search tool for ftp sites, now superseded by Web search engines.

attribute. One of three characteristics of a **tag (element)**. Some are required and some optional. Some take values.

background. An overall colour for a Web page which can be defined by a colour statement (BGCOLOR = "RED") or an image file (BACKGROUND = "image1.gif"). Note US spelling of colour.

bandwidth. Used loosely to mean the amount of traffic a server or carrying line can handle, and therefore its speed.

browser. A program which reads and displays HTML documents (Web pages). Graphical browsers include Netscape, Internet Explorer and Mosaic. Non-graphical browsers include Lynx. At the last count there were 63.

CGI. Common Gateway Interface. The format for sending information from browsers to servers using forms or queries in HTML documents.

client. A computer connected to a server, often at a great distance.

CompuServe. The world's second-largest on-line service provider (after AOL).

Cyberspace. A term coined by William Gibson in his novel *Neuromancer* to describe a shared virtual reality environment, now more loosely used to mean the totality of what is on the Internet.

DNS. Domain Name System – every Internet site has a unique DNS (in the form of 123.456.789.368) which is hard to remember, so **domain names** are used.

document. The HTML that constitutes a Web page.

domain name. A unique identifier of an Internet site, like a street address, whereas the DNS is like a post code.

DTD. Document Type Definition. The specification of HTML.

element. A component of the document type definition (**DTD**) which contains HTML, markups, also called a **tag** and containing **attributes**, types and content.

e-mail. Electronic mail. Everyone using the Internet has an e-mail address, which always includes the @ symbol (e.g. j.smith@ microsoft.com).

FTP (or ftp). File Transfer Protocol – more than a protocol, more a mechanism for moving files between Internet sites. FTP log-in always requires a password but this is often the word 'anonymous', hence 'anonymous ftp sites'.

GIF. Graphics Information File – the commonest (with JPEG) image format on the Web. GIFs can be animated – essentially a series of GIFs which load one on top of another.

HotJava. A Web browser from Sun Microsystems, authors of the **Java** language.

hotspot. See **image map**.

HTML. HyperText Markup Language, a specific example of **SGML**.

HTTP. HyperText Transfer Protocol – an object-oriented protocol used by Web servers.

hypertext. A mechanism for allowing text, graphics, etc. links to other locations, usually on a mouse link.

image map. A graphic containing one or more areas (**hot spots**) of clickable links.

interlacing. A method for loading GIFs and JPEGs which handles them in stages, speeding download times.

Internet. If you have to look it up, you shouldn't be reading this book.

Internet Explorer. Microsoft's Web browser.

Java. Sun Microsystems' new **platform-dependent** programming language which will revolutionise not only the Web but all computing. Primarily it delivers **applets** to perform special functions within Web pages, but this could be the way all software is written soon. Netscape is Java-compatible and Internet Explorer will be.

JPEG. Joint Photographic Experts Group and the graphic format it has defined – is compressible format especially useful for photographs (usually with the filename extension .jpg).

Lycos. One of the best Web search engines which also carried adverts.

mailing lists. Lists of addresses, useful for e-mail marketing campaigns. A good source of these is *http://catalog.com/vivian/interest-group-search.html*.

markup. Information for the browser which tells it how to display the HTML data. There are four different kinds: descriptive markup (**tags**), references, processing instructions and markup declarations.

MIME. Multipurpose Internet Mail Extensions – the standard method for attaching non-text files to e-mail and sending it between computers, basically by turning into (unreadable) text. A Web browser will pair a MIME type with the right software for running it.

Mosaic. The first, and now largely superseded, Web browser. There are different versions of Mosaic, including Spry, owned by **CompuServe**. Mosaic may all but disappear when CompuServe changes to a version of Internet.

NCSA. National Center for Supercomputer Applications – the US academic institution where much of the good work on computers happens. NCSA invented **Mosaic**.

net, the net. The Internet.

Netscape. Netscape Communications, makers of Navigator, the most popular browser.

Platform-independent. A program or other data which will operate on any computer, whether Mac, PC, UNIX, or whatever.

POP. Point Of Presence – a local computer where a user can dial in to get remote access to a server further away.

POP. Post Office Protocol – the way e-mail software gets mail from a server.

SGML. Standard Generalized Markup Language – **HTML** is a specific example of this.

tag. Descriptive markup around an **element**. There are two kinds, < Start > and < /End > .

telnet. A method of establishing direct (and private) connections between two computers on the Internet.

URI. Universal Resource Identifier.

URL. Universal Resource Locator – a naming system for all resources available on the Web – Web pages, sites, server, etc. A URL has up to six components, the first two being essential. Example: *http://info.uae.ac.uk:80/pages/homepage.htm#top*

1. Protocol (http:// or ftp://) – identifies the method used to access the data.
2. Domain name (info.uae.ac.uk) – the server holding the information. Common suffixes are co or com (in the USA) – a company; ac or deu (USA) – a university; gov – government body; mil – US military; net – a service provider; org – non-profit organisation (e.g. a charity). The domain name may also have a country identifier such as uk or fi (Finland).
3. Port address (usually :80) – and usually omitted.
4. Directory path (/pages/) – where on the server the files are located.
5. Object (homepage.htm) – the actual Web page or other resource.
6. Spot (#top) – a specific place in the Web page, requiring an anchor.

webmaster or webmeister. A job title that didn't exist a few short years ago – a constructor, organiser and fount of all wisdom on Web pages. Once a lonely, sad individual working away at midnight in a deserted computer room, the webmeister is now a highly regarded and well-paid position in many large companies.

WWW (the Web). The World-Wide Web, one component of the Internet and the most popular. It allows graphical content.

Index

MANAGING YOUR FIRST COMPUTER
How to perform core tasks and go on to achieve proficiency

Carol Dolman and Marcus Saunders

Anyone new to the world of computers can expect to be baffled by the huge array of equipment, programs, books, and above all, the mind-boggling jargon that goes with the territory. How much do you need to know to use a computer effectively? This book will guide the first-time or inexperienced user simply and painlessly towards making use of all major applications in the shortest possible time. With clear illustrations and practical exercises, the reader will be using their computer effectively right from the start. Carol Dolman and Marcus Saunders are both qualified computer technicians who have worked with computers since 1979. They run their own computer business, servicing and installing computer systems, and specialise in instructing those new to computing.

144pp. illus. 1 85703 293 4.

USING THE INTERNET
How to make the most of the information superhighway

Graham Jones

Soon, nearly everyone in the developed world will have access to the Internet. This book shows you how and where to begin. Unlike other books on the 'Net', this down-to-earth practical guide, now in its second edition, will really help you to get onto the Net and start exploring the new 'information superhighway'. Using case examples, it illustrates some of the many benefits the Internet can bring, and the personal, business or educational goals you can achieve. Graham Jones is a leading business consultant and writer. He is the author of *How to Manage Computers at Work* in this series, and has contributed to many computer magazines. He runs his own publishing business that depends on the Internet for up-to-date information.

128pp. illus. 1 85703 237 3. 2nd edition.

DESIGNING FOR DESKTOP PUBLISHING
How to create clear and effective documents with your DTP program

Diane Hudson

Creating a document is much like putting together a jigsaw puzzle. It will only be finished when all the pieces are in the right place. Desktop publishing is the art of combining written skills together with design skills to produce eye-catching documents on your PC. Whether you want to produce a newsletter for your club or society, or a sales brochure for your business, many of the same rules apply. This book will show you the techniques used for producing attractive and effective documents for a variety of uses. Diane Hudson is a technical author, writing user manuals and on-line Help for computer software.

144pp. illus. 1 85703 279 9.

BUYING A PERSONAL COMPUTER
How to choose the right equipment to meet your needs

Allen Brown

Many thousands of personal computers (PCs) are sold annually and they are becoming general purpose, everyday tools. Buying a PC for the first time represents a significant financial outlay. This book, now in a fully updated second edition, will help potential buyers in their choice of PC, their selection of peripherals, and appropriate software. It aims to be precise, yet with sufficient information to enable a new user to understand a PC specification and to ensure that it will be adequate for their needs. It will also provide information on applications that the buyer may be thinking of for the future. Dr Allen Brown is a Senior Lecturer in Electronics in the School of Applied Sciences at Anglia Polytechnic University, Cambridge.

176pp. illus. 1 85703 233 0. 2nd edition.

DOING BUSINESS ON THE INTERNET
How to use the new technology to win a competitive edge

Graham Jones

If you would like to explore the Internet, but are not quite sure where to start, this is the book for you. Act now, and make sure you start taking advantage of what this amazing new technology has to offer every business today. Graham Jones runs a specialist newsletter and desktop publishing business, and has many years' experience of using the Internet in his own business dealings. He is also author of *How to Manage Computers at Work* in this series.

120pp. illus. 1 85703 364 7.

HOW TO WRITE & SELL COMPUTER SOFTWARE
A practical guide to creating and marketing software ideas

Stephen Harding

This book is for people who want to write and sell their own software, either to make a living or just a useful part-time income. From business software to computer games, this book explains how to identify and research the market, how to plan and prepare a quality software product for launch, how to package, advertise and distribute your product, how to attract and stimulate customer interest and, most important of all, how to sell it, build a customer base and operate a successful and professional software business.

160pp. illus. 1 85703 214 4.